The world's best-selling graphics software and winner of over 200 first place international awards, CorelDRAW is renowned for its ease of use, incredible value and outstanding features! CorelDRAW lets your imagination soar. Precision type control, superb drawing power and amazing special effects make it easy for anyone to create dynamic desktop documents, lively illustrations and colorful presentations. This extraordinary graphics software package also includes hundreds of fonts and thousands of clipart images and symbols. CorelDRAW is network ready and multilingual.

An annual publication of
Corel Corporation

Corel Corporation
1600 Carling Avenue
Ottawa, Ontario
Canada K1Z 8R7

Tel:(613) 728-8200
Fax:(613) 728-2891

President and CEO
Dr. Michael C.J. Cowpland

Designed by:
Corel Design Department

Copyright © 1995

The world is moving so fast these days that the man who says it can't be done is generally interrupted by someone doing it.

Elbert Hubbard (1856-1915)

As children, we never questioned our capabilities or aspirations. When we painted the sun, the finished result was in our minds a true-to-life representation. We dressed up in our parents' old clothes and were suddenly transformed from child to adult. We told funny stories and instantly commanded an audience. In our childlike innocence, we had not yet conceptualized a world where human ambitions and desires could be held back by human limitations.

Something akin to our childhood faith in human ability seems to have infiltrated the spirit of the 90's. Indeed, as the boundaries of human potential and progress become less defined, there's simply no predicting what historical breakthroughs lie just around the corner. New developments in the technological world in particular have opened exciting doors in our personal and professional lives. Today, with the click of a mouse we communicate with the world, and with technology advancing by such leaps and bounds, yesterday's perceived boundaries are quickly becoming tomorrow's stepping stones.

It is certainly unlikely that the words "can't be done" ever crossed the lips of the founder of Corel Corporation. Dr. Michael Cowpland realized very early in his career that the twentieth century mind both demands and thrives on progress, and that computer users worldwide would always require software tools that could keep pace with their professional needs and boundless creativity. Since its inception, Corel has been committed to providing its millions of faithful users with faster and more powerful versions of its software products. The images contained in this unique coffee-table book and companion CD-ROM, selected from over 7,800 entries submitted by Corel software users worldwide, bear witness to that faith and that commitment.

Appropriately enough, this year's Sixth Annual Corel World Design Contest provided a wonderful opportunity for the company's Director of Sales and Marketing, Mr. Arlen Bartsch, to deliver a timely retrospective on Corel's flagship product. His message was simple, but powerfully clear—CorelDRAW as we know it today has come a long way since CorelDRAW Version 1. And it is surely no coincidence that with each passing year the images in the Corel *ArtShow* series appear to grow more intricate and more compellingly beautiful than ever before.

The Sixth Annual Corel World Design Contest, held in conjunction with the much-anticipated launch of CorelDRAW 6 for Windows 95, was for all who participated a very memorable evening.

Held at the National Arts Centre in Ottawa, attendees at this year's "Academy Awards of Graphics" witnessed a superior selection of computer-generated art and were treated to a unique and beautifully choreographed modern dance extravaganza.

Presided over by Corel President, Dr. Michael Cowpland and Manager of Media Relations, Fiona Rochester, the audience cheered as the Grand Prize and Best of Show winners were announced. The Best of Show winner, also a Grand Prize winner in the Goodwill Poster category, was a particularly popular choice. Trophies and generous prize packages were presented to each winner and a total of almost $150,000 was donated to six international charities. The official launch of CorelDRAW 6 was now only minutes away.

Dancers, weaving long, flowing lengths of purple and yellow silk ribbon in and out of the mist-enshrouded air, added wonderfully to the palpable air of anticipation. And as the lithe figures whirled and looped their ribbons around an enormous silk-sheathed box, one could feel the undercurrent of excitement grow more intense—the moment everyone had been waiting for was drawing nearer.

And the audience was not to be disappointed. The silk veil fell to the floor, and a new CorelDRAW box rose spectacularly against a dazzling backdrop of stunning sound and lighting effects. CorelDRAW 6 was officially launched.

For you the reader, these words and accompanying photographs will only partly convey the sense of excitement that charged the air that August evening. However, once you have explored the wonderful images contained within these pages, we feel confident that you will come to understand what worthy showcases of international artistic talent the Corel World Design Contest and its culmination, the *ArtShow* series, truly are.

Alt om Data, Editor-in-Chief, *Torben Okholm*

Anzai! Inc., President, *Tom Anzai*

Bell Canada, President/Chief Executive Officer, *John McLennan*

Bitstream Inc., Director of Emerging Technologies, *Jim Welch*

Blake, Cassels & Graydon, Sec. Treasurer of Corel Corp., *Paul LaBarge*

Bretton Woods, Chairman, *Bruce Firestone*

Mark Brownstein, **Freelance Reviewer**

BYTE, Editor-in-Chief, *Rafe Needleman*

c/net online, Editor-in-Chief, *Christopher Barr*

Canadian Advanced Technology, President, *John Reid*

Canon Canada, Product Support Manager, *Steve Mission*

Capital, Editor, *Aenne Riesenberg*

Carleton University, President, *Robin Farquhar*

CBC News, Reporter, *Danny Globerman*

CD-ROM Multimedia, Editor-in-Chief, Publisher, *Eyo Sama*

CD-ROM Today, Editor-in-Chief, *Daniel Tynan*

CHIP, Assistant Editor-in-Chief, *Gerhard Bader*

Cinema One Productions, President, *Bob Kovoloff*

City of Ottawa, Mayor of Ottawa, *Jacquelin Holzman*

City of Rockcliffe, Mayor of Rockcliffe, *Patrick Murray*

CJOH TV, Assignment Editor, *Paul Brent*

Client Center Training, Owner, *Carole Crone*

Coca-Cola Corporation, Senior Engineer, *Steve Cousins*

Cognos, President/COO, *Ron Zambonini*

Computer Artist, Associate Editor, *Nancy Hitchcock*

Computer City, President, *Alan C. Bush*

Computer Life, Editor-in-Chief, *John Dickinson*

Computer Life, News Editor, *Jan Howell*

Computer Magazine, Freelance, *Luc Elst*

Computer Paper, Editor, *Graeme Bennett*

Computer Paper, Editor, *Jeff Evans*

Computer! Totaal, News Editor, *Berend Harmsen*

Computing Canada, Features Editor, *Suzanne Wintrob*

Corel Corporation, President & CEO, *Dr. Michael Cowpland*

Corel Corporation, Member of the Board, *Hon. William Davis*

Corel Corporation, Member of the Board, *Sir Anthony Jolliffe, GBE*

Corel Corporation, Member of the Board, *Ben Webster*

Corel Corporation, Member of the Board, *Lyle Blair*

Corel Magazine, Editor, *Scott Campbell*

CorelNet, Webmaster, *Chris Dickman*

Christine Cowpland

Paula Cowpland

Daily Telegraph, Innovations, *Sue Taylor*

Decision Micro, Editor, *Pascal Langlet*

Desktop Design, President, *Jim Maivald*

Diamond Multimedia, President, *William Schroeder*

Digital Equipment Corp., VP/Worldwide Marketing, *Joseph Cannizzaro*

Digital Equipment of Canada, PC Technical Sales Rep., *Al Veenema*

Discover Magazine, Editor-in-Chief, *Paul Hoffman*

DMV Sonderpublikationen/DOS Extra, Editor-in-Chief, *Marina Baader*

DTP Media, Managing Director, *Thomas Bauer*

Mike Duffy, **Host of Sunday Edition - BBS**

Eastman Kodak, Business Development Executive, *Jack McWilliams*

Egeland, Wood & Zuber, President, *Elizabeth Wood*

Egghead Software, Vice-President of Merchandise, *Pete Janssen*

EiWei EDV Journalisten, Freelance, *Helge Weickardt*

Embassy of Spain, Ambassador, *Jose Luis Pardos*

Phil Evans, **Freelance**

Family PC, Editor-in-Chief, *Robin Raskin*

Don Frost, **Sculptor**

Bronwyn Fryer, **Freelance**

Ottawa General Hospital, Surgeon, *JP Desjardins MD FRCS(C)*

Graphic Design USA, Editor/Co-Publisher, *Gordon Kaye*

Graphic Presentations, Senior Designer, *Blake Barr*

Hewlett-Packard Company, ISV Program Manager, *Dave Stewart*

Hewlett-Packard, Learning Product Engineer, *Jerry Day*

Home Office Computing, Senior Editor, *Susie Rich*

HSC Software, Chairman/CEO, *John Wilczak*

David Huss, **Author**

IBIS, President, *Mike Schneider*

IDG - Latin America, Editor, *Margarita Alvarez*

IKOY Architects, *Dominique McEwan*

JUDGES

IKOY Architects, *Ron Keenberg*
Info-Tech Magazine, Publisher/Editor, *Alain Thibault*
InfoCanada Reseller World, Editor, *Grace Casselman*
Inset Systems, Business Development Director, *Michael Kaltschnee*
Inter Com International, President, *Jim Karney*
Iomega, Director of Western Sales, *Gary Jones*
Sean James
Kapital, Business Editor, *Permatin Fosmark*
Aili Kurtis, **Artist**
Le Devoir, Editor, *Andre Salwyn*
Lovelady Consulting, Exec. Dir. Ventura User Exchange, *Carol Lovelady*
Marketing Computers, Editor, *David Evans*
Matrox, Communication Manager, *Mary Ellen Power*
MC Microcomputer, Director, *Massimo Truscelli*
Mikrodatorn, Editor-in-Chief, *Mats Hultgren*
National Gallery of Canada, Director, *Dr. Shirley Thompson*
New Media, Executive Editor/Products, *Becky Waring*
OC EDCO, President/General Manager, *Keith McGruer*
Osler, Hoskin & Harcourt, Senior Partner, *Kent Plumley*
Ottawa Carleton Research Inst., President, *Gerry Turcotte*
Ottawa SUN, Business Editor, *Stuart McCarthy*
PC Labs, Principal, *Ted Vegvari*
PC Letter, Contributing Editor, *Lisa Halliday*
PC Letter, Editor/Publisher, *David Coursey*
PC Anwender, Editor, *Michael A. Schmithäuser*
PC Hemma - Sweden, Editor-in-Chief, *Per-Otto Lekare*
PC Magazine, Contributing Editor, *John Quain*
PC Magazine, Director, *Sergio Mello-Grand*
PC Magazine, Editor-in-Chief, VP, *Michael Miller*
PC Media - Spain, Mexico, Arg., President, Editorial House, *Antonio Ferrer*
PC Plus, Associate Editor, *Simon Williams*
PC Pro, Editor, *Derek Cohen*
PC Welt, Assistant Editor-in-Chief, *Heiderose Witte*
PC World, Senior Associate Editor, *Christina Wood*
PC/Computing, Editor-in-Chief, *John Zilber*
PC/Computing, Executive Editor, *Wendy Taylor*
Personal Computer Magazine, Editor, *Branko Djakovic*

Personal Computing - Mexico, Associate Editor, *Javier Matuk*
Playboy Enterprises, Executive Vice-President, *Richard Rosenzweig*
Polaroid Corporation, Marketing Program Manager, *Mary Ann Lidrbauch*
Pressebüro Europa, Editor-in-Chief, *Ernst Demianiuk*
R. Altman & Associates, Author/Consultant, *Rick Altman*
Regional Municipality of Ottawa-Carleton, Regional Chairman, *Peter Clark*
Retlab Graphics Inc., President, *Pradahn Balter*
Eric-Jan Royen, **Freelance**
ROZZ Fashion, *Marilyn Cowpland*
SMART, Editor, *David English*
Softbank Exposition, VP Consumer Events, *Michael Edelhart*
Summagraphics, Product Manager, *Sam Perkins*
Super PC - Spain, Editor, *Luis Jorge Garcia*
Tagline VPU UK, Production Editor, *Edward Brown*
Technology Forum Inc., Executive Director, *Priscilla Tate*
Theta Data, President of ACAD, *Randy Tobin*
Time, Inc., Manager, Information Technology, *John Butler*
Time, Inc., Vice-President Information Technology, *Paul Zazzera*
Titokone - Finland, Editor-in-Chief, *Jukka Nortio*
Toronto Computes/Toronto Star, Contributing Editor, *Myles White*
Toronto Star, Technology Editor, *Rob Wright*
University of Ottawa, The Rector, *Marcel Hamelin*
Unleashed Productions, President, *Foster Coburn III*
Unleashed Productions, Vice-President, *Peter McCormick*
Vet's Choice, Advertising Manager, *Ryan Villiers-Furze*
Wacom Technology Corporation, Senior Marketing Manager, *Jeffrey Nichols*
Westin Hotel, General Manager, *Jim Hill*
What PC?, Editor, *Mick Andon*
WIN, Assistant Editor-in-Chief, *Elke Huff*
Windows Magazine, Executive Editor, *Michael Elgan*
Windows Magazine, Writer, *Jim Bell*
Windows News, News Editor, *Annie Lichner*
Windows Sources, Senior Editor, *Lori Grunin*
Wohl Associates, President, Editor & Publisher, *Amy Wohl*
Xerox Canada, Color Sales Specialist, *Bill Guthrie*
Ziff-Davis Labs, Executive Director, *Bob Kane*

PRIZES AND SPONSORS

Best of Show

The overall Best of Show winner was selected from the monthly category Grand Prize winners and the annual categories of Goodwill Poster, Corel Professional Photos, Best of the Americas and Best of Europe and the Rest of the World. The Best of Show winner received $150,000 in cash and prizes.

Best of Show Prize Package:

- $50,000 cash
- Xerox MagestiK Color Series printer valued at $70,000
- Summagraphics SummaChrome Imaging System valued at $30,000

Grand Prizes

10 Grand Prize winners were selected from the monthly, Goodwill Poster, Corel Professional Photos, Corel VENTURA and CorelMOVE categories. Each winner was awarded $21,000 in prizes.

Grand Prize Package:

- MGA Impression Plus graphics accelerator board
- Seagate hard drive
- DECpc Lpx Series Pentium computer
- Nanao FlexiScan F560iW 17" monitor
- Polaroid SprintScan 35 slide scanner
- Tektronix Phaser 220e printer
- HP ScanJet IIex scanner
- Bernoulli MultiDisk 150 removable disk drive
- NEC MultiSpin 3Xe CD-ROM drive
- 200 Corel Professional Photos

2 Grand Prize winners were selected from the 14 global finalists. They were awarded $21,000 in prizes.

Best of the Americas Prize Package:

- Xerox 4900 color laser printer
- DCS 20 digital camera

Best of Europe and the Rest of the World Prize Package:

- Canon CJ10 desktop color printer/scanner/copier
- NEC 21" color 6FGp monitor
- 150 Corel Professional Photos

Monthly Category Winners

48 winners were selected from the 6 monthly categories and awarded $5,000 in prizes. Monthly winners were eligible for Grand Prizes.

Monthly Prize Package:

- Kai's Power Tools 2.0
- ArtPad 4 x 5 graphics tablet
- HiJack PRO file conversion
- PIXAR "One Twenty Eight" CD-ROM
- Kodak Arrange-It Photo CD software
- HP DeskJet 560C printer
- ProSound multimedia speakers
- Bitstream Typeface Library
- trueSpace 3D software
- TMC-1610MC SCSI kit
- National Association of Desktop Artists membership
- CorelSCSI Version 2
- 25 Corel Professional Photos

Global Finalists

14 finalists were selected from the 500 Honorable Mentions chosen throughout the year. The finalists were awarded $2,500 and were eligible for Best of the Americas and Best of Europe and the Rest of the World Grand Prizes.

Global Prize Packages:

- UD1212RP graphics tablet
- Visual Reality 3D product suite
- Stealth 64 graphics card
- Sound Blaster 16 Value Edition
- 25 Corel Professional Photos

PRIZES AND SPONSORS

Canon NANAO NEC Polaroid

XEROX  Summagraphics Seagate

All product and company names are
trademarks or registered trademarks of
their respective companies.

Best of Show

Radim Mojzis
Czech Republic

There are no limits when using CorelDRAW, says this year's Best of Show winner. *The Drops of Life* was originally created for T-shirts for the Czech Red Cross and also won the Goodwill Poster category in this year's Corel World Design Contest. CorelDRAW, Corel PHOTO-PAINT and CorelTRACE were all used to seamlessly blend textures, scanned images and different fountain and uniform fills in this poster urging people to give blood. At his one-man design studio in Vsetin, Czech Republic, Mojzis creates a variety of promotional items, including billboards, brochures and greeting cards—all with the help of CorelDRAW, which he calls the most "friendly" graphics program on the market!

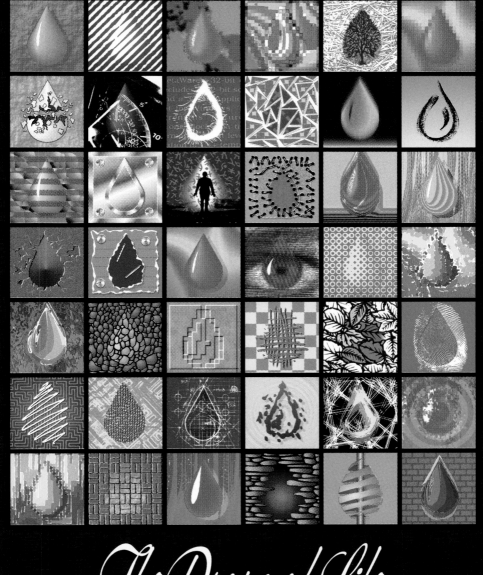

The Drops of Life

Gift of Blood - Gift of Life ✚ Different ways to Help

CZECH RED CROSS

Grand Prize

PEOPLE, PLANTS AND ANIMALS

Robert Travers
Canada

This talented designer got a taste for his future career when, as a child, he began drawing portraits to compete with an older brother who liked to draw Mickey Mouse! This multi-layered portrait, called *Window Shopping*, was accomplished using two base drawings —the painting and the reflection. They both had their beginnings in CorelDRAW 4 and were then edited in Corel PHOTO-PAINT to add realism and atmosphere. One corner of the frame was drawn and then mirrored. All the separate pieces were eventually combined and enveloped slightly to make the portrait converge at the top. Rectangles from CorelDRAW were welded together to form the reflection of the building. The word "GALERIE" was added later with CorelDRAW 5. This gifted artist has also won previous Corel World Design Contest awards.

Grand Prize

LANDSCAPES, LANDMARKS AND ABSTRACTS

John M. Morris
U.S.A.

This charming winter scene was the result of the designer's efforts to produce a computer illustration that did not resemble a typical computer graphic. Not only does *Reflections* refer to the image on the windowpane, it also urges viewers to "reflect" on their childhood memories. The illustration was produced using five major vector elements which were then rendered using as many CorelDRAW 5 features as possible. The chipmunk and bluebird were both taken from CorelDRAW clipart and slightly modified. The background scene was taken from the Corel "Scenics" Photo CD and the window was rendered in CorelDRAW and exported to Corel PHOTO-PAINT. The two children were scanned from 35mm slides and combined with the export file. An accomplished illustrator with 25 years experience, Morris also won two Awards of Excellence in the 1993 Corel World Design Contest.

Grand Prize

PRODUCT ILLUSTRATION

Michael Koester
Germany

The inspiration for this detailed isometric view of a Nikon F-801 35mm camera began with a shopping trip! The designer wanted to buy a camera and went to the library to do some research before choosing one. He looked at a book containing a black-and-white line drawing of a camera cut in half so that the parts were visible. The challenge was to recreate the same effect in color using computer graphics software. The final image is very precise, with each part appearing in the correct position with true proportions. Each little detail contains at least one gradient fill and not surprisingly, *F-801* took an exhausting seven months to create on the artist's 386-40 computer.

Grand Prize

PAGE LAYOUT AND DESIGN

Theodor Ushev
Bulgaria

This talented artist has participated in graphic design exhibitions and competitions all over the world. His work also won him a Grand Prize in last year's Corel World Design Contest in the same category. This particular design, called *Radio 3*, was conceived as a postcard to be sent to Radio Bulgaria listeners across the globe. The initial sketch of this eclectic blend of images, patterns and colors was scanned and traced with CorelTRACE and then manipulated and enhanced using CorelDRAW 5.

Grand Prize

MAY • CATEGORY WINNER

CORPORATE IDENTIFICATION

This double Grand Prize and Best of Show winning artist created *Aerobic Logo* for a sports equipment company. He began his career as a designer in an advertising company using CorelDRAW 2. The silhouette figure in this supremely clean design was created by hand, then scanned and traced. CorelDRAW applications were used to help correct and enhance the figure and give the whole design a sense of movement and energy. The overall look and feel of the design was solidified with the addition of the stylish typography.

Radim Mojzis

Czech Republic

aerobic

EQUIPMENT FOR MAN

Grand Prize

SPECIALTY AND LEISURE

Amedeo Gigli
Italy

In a career spanning almost 50 years, this experienced illustrator for multinational publicity agencies only began using CorelDRAW three years ago. His *Maserati* design showcases the beauty and history of one of Italy's most prestigious automobile companies. With the tools available in CorelDRAW 3 and CorelDRAW 5, he blended objects and colors, adding customized linear and radial fills following the object's dimensions and orientation. Rainbow effects were used to represent light sources and transparency lenses added depth and lighting to the body of the car, producing a realistic look.

Amedio Gigli was unable to attend this year's "Academy Awards of Graphics" Gala, but his son Alessio (pictured), was happy to accept the Grand Prize Award on his behalf!

MASERATI 4CL "16 valvole"

MASERATI
50
years ago

Driver: TAZIO NUVOLARI - 1946

Grand Prize

CATEGORY ◆ WINNER

COREL PROFESSIONAL PHOTOS

Matthias Gleirscher
Austria

This very talented artist has only been using computers for three years. He discovered CorelDRAW 3 in the first year and has just recently started using CorelDRAW 5. *Different Eyes*, a combination wolf/woman portrait, was created by blending two Corel Professional Photos—from the "Wolves" and "Sunset and Sunrise" series—with one of the artist's own photo images. Gleirscher writes that he can't wait to work with CorelDRAW 6!

Grand Prize

Valorie Lennox
Canada

Dragon Lord, an amazing 15th-century style animated medieval manuscript, was created using CorelDRAW, Corel PHOTO-PAINT and CorelMOVE. All of the visual elements—39 actors and 21 props—were created in one program or by using a combination of the three. A CorelDRAW blend of two custom shades for the authentic-looking "vellum" background lends a touch of antiquity to this beautiful design. CorelDRAW also helped the artist create the "Dragon Skin" texture fill used for the dragon wings. Craft clay, cardboard and toys served as photographic models for Lennox's engaging dragon actors, the prints of which were then imported via hand scanner and customized in Corel PHOTO-PAINT. This innovative designer also created a fade in/fade out effect using the morph command in CorelMOVE. To top it all off, the soundtrack is an ancient Celtic tune, adding to the medieval feel of the manuscript.

Dragon Lord

An animated manuscript

Once upon a valley fair

A fearsome dragon ruled all there

Black vapour billowed

His flame-laced breath seared the air

Of crops and cattle he took a share

But in that valley no man dare

To challenge the Dragon Lord

Grand Prize

COREL VENTURA/PUBLISHING

Jim Bisakowski/Lee Gabel
Canada

This dynamic duo work together at a desktop publishing company in Victoria, British Columbia. The 1994 *Commonwealth Games Broadcasters Handbook and Final Report* offered the perfect forum to show off the versatility of Corel VENTURA. The entire layout was produced with Corel VENTURA 5, with illustrations from CorelDRAW 5. One of the goals for the report was elegance, achieved through a liberal use of white space and the decision to keep the text mirrored in the center of each double-page spread. The inside front covers were created using CorelDRAW 5's transparency lens feature and careful attention was paid to font selection. Bisakowski, the company owner, and Gabel, the project manager, are both extremely pleased with Corel VENTURA, and say that 95% of all their work is produced with Corel products!

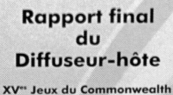

Grand Prize

CATEGORY ◆ WINNER

ℬEST OF THE AMERICAS

Silvio Martins Alegre
Brazil

This futuristic design comes from an artist who acquired his first personal computer in 1993. Since correct perspective is key to the success of *Far Away*, a profile view of the station first had to be created. The massive red planet was created in Corel PHOTO-PAINT using the blend, airbrush and smear tools. The brightly-colored planet background with its large "storm spots" contrasts with the clean, sharp lines of the space station. Remarkable attention to detail gives the station its realistic look, including walkways, docking bays, lights, windows and surface paneling. The finely-detailed space station was created in CorelDRAW, after an extensive preparation process.

Grand Prize

CATEGORY◆WINNER

BEST OF EUROPE AND THE REST OF THE WORLD

Alexandre Kojouchner
Ukraine

This enchanting image was created exclusively in CorelDRAW, with each portion drawn and colored separately. The artistic style is fanciful and the designer writes that he was inspired by the work of artist Vladimir Fomin. Kojouchner used a combination of bold, uneven strokes and bright colors to evoke a feeling of whimsy, while the fine details and a variety of textures give *Artist* its charm and warmth. The designer has only been working with CorelDRAW for a year and writes that he definitely plans to participate in future Corel World Design Contests!

Alexandre Kojouchner was unable to attend this year's "Academy Awards of Graphics" Gala.

SEPTEMBER • CATEGORY WINNER

Jerry Brown, U.S.A.

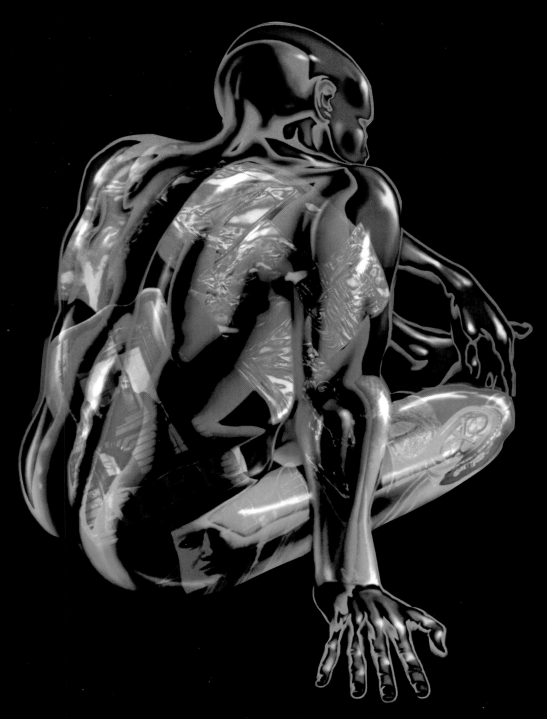

OCTOBER ◆ CATEGORY WINNER

Robert Travers, Canada

DECEMBER ◆ CATEGORY WINNER

Huan Le Tran, Canada

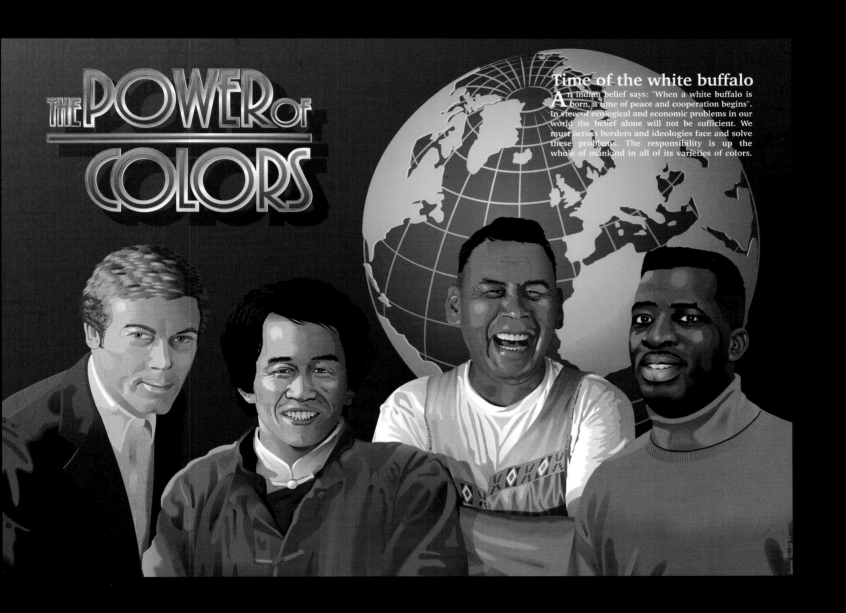

THE POWER OF COLORS

Time of the white buffalo
An indian belief says: "When a white buffalo is born, a time of peace and cooperation begins". In view of ecological and economic problems in our world the belief alone will not be sufficient. We must across borders and ideologies face and solve these problems. The responsibility is up the whole of mankind in all of its varieties of colors.

JANUARY ◆ CATEGORY WINNER

Andreas Sewald, Germany

27

WINDOW ON WILDLIFE

FEBRUARY ◆ CATEGORY WINNER

Ceri Lines, Taiwan

MARCH/APRIL ◆ CATEGORY WINNER

Georgina Curry/Gerry Moss, U.S.A.

MAY • CATEGORY WINNER

Huan Le Tran, Canada

SEPTEMBER ◆ CATEGORY WINNER

Gerry Wilson, U.S.A.

$\mathcal{L}$ANDSCAPES, LANDMARKS AND ABSTRACTS

OCTOBER ◆ CATEGORY WINNER

Gustavo A. Ortiz Serrano, Columbia

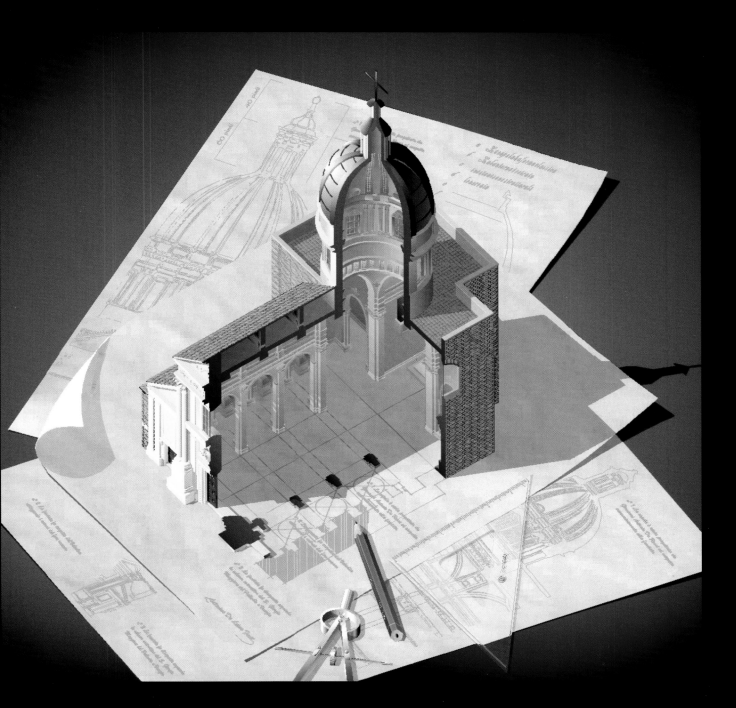

NOVEMBER ◆ CATEGORY WINNER

Antonio De Leo, Italy

DECEMBER ◆ CATEGORY WINNER

Jerry Brown, U.S.A.

34

JANUARY ◆ CATEGORY WINNER

Fabio Gargitter, Brazil

*L*ANDSCAPES, LANDMARKS AND ABSTRACTS

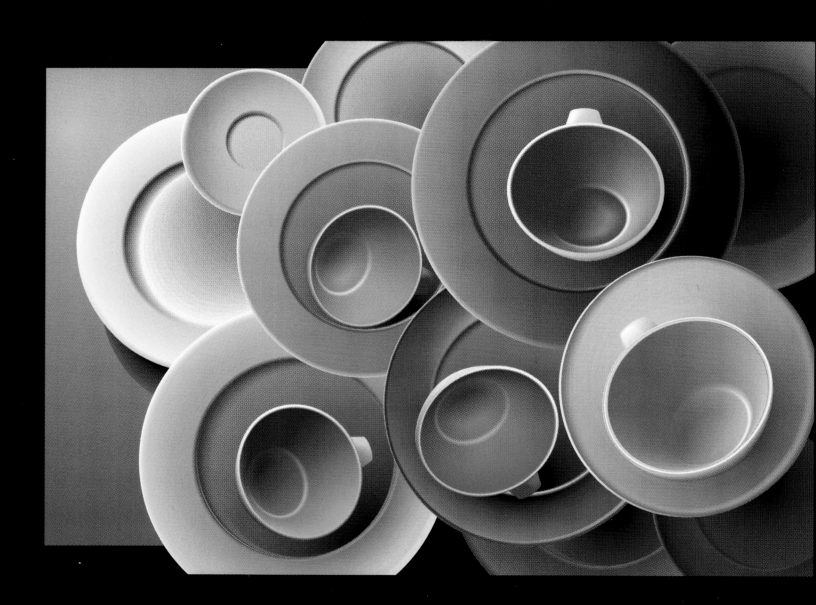

FEBRUARY ◆ CATEGORY WINNER

Tomasz Wawrzyczek, Poland

MARCH/APRIL ◆ CATEGORY WINNER

Mathew Lecher, U.S.A.

PRODUCT ILLUSTRATION

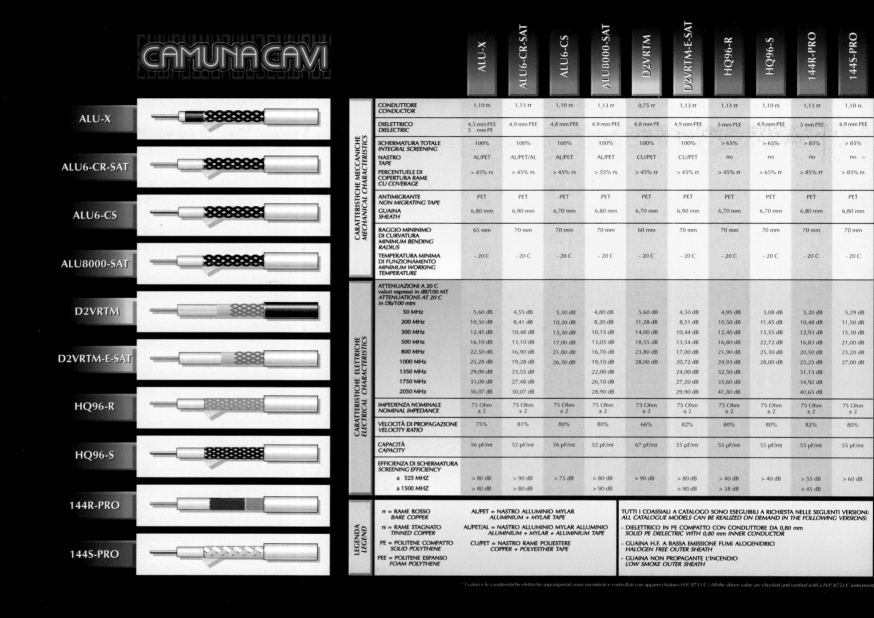

CAMUNACAVI

ALU-X
ALU6-CR-SAT
ALU6-CS
ALU8000-SAT
D2VRTM
D2VRTM-E-SAT
HQ96-R
HQ96-S
144R-PRO
144S-PRO

CARATTERISTICHE MECCANICHE / MECHANICAL CHARACTERISTICS

	ALU-X	ALU6-CR-SAT	ALU6-CS	ALU8000-SAT	D2VRTM	D2VRTM-E-SAT	HQ96-R	HQ96-S	144R-PRO	144S-PRO
CONDUTTORE / CONDUCTOR	1,10 rs	1,13 rr	1,10 rs	1,13 rr	0,75 rr	1,13 rr	1,13 rr	1,10 rs	1,13 rr	1,10 rs
DIELETTRICO / DIELECTRIC	4,5 mm PEE 5 mm PE	4,9 mm PEE	4,8 mm PEE	4,9 mm PEE	4,8 mm PE	4,9 mm PEE	5 mm PEE	4,9 mm PEE	5 mm PEE	4,9 mm PEE
SCHERMATURA TOTALE / INTEGRAL SCREENING	100%	100%	100%	100%	100%	100%	> 65%	> 65%	> 85%	> 85%
NASTRO / TAPE	AL/PET	AL/PET/AL	AL/PET	AL/PET	CU/PET	CU/PET	no	no	no	no
PERCENTUELE DI COPERTURA RAME / CU COVERAGE	> 45% rs	> 45% rs	> 45% rs	> 55% rs	> 45% rr	> 45% rr	> 45% rr	> 65% rr	> 85% rr	> 85% rs
ANTIMIGRANTE / NON MIGRATING TAPE	PET	PET	PET	PET	PET	PET	PET	PET	PET	PET
GUAINA / SHEATH	6,80 mm	6,90 mm	6,70 mm	6,80 mm	6,70 mm	6,90 mm	6,70 mm	6,70 mm	6,80 mm	6,80 mm
RAGGIO MININIMO DI CURVATURA / MINIMUM BENDING RADIUS	65 mm	70 mm	70 mm	70 mm	60 mm	70 mm	70 mm	70 mm	70 mm	70 mm
TEMPERATURA MINIMA DI FUNZIONAMENTO / MINIMUM WORKING TEMPERATURE	- 20 C	- 20 C	- 20 C	- 20 C	- 20 C	- 20 C	- 20 C	- 20 C	- 20 C	- 20 C

CARATTERISTICHE ELETTRICHE / ELECTRICAL CHARACTERISTICS

ATTENUAZIONI A 20 C valori espressi in dB/100 MT / ATTENUATIONS AT 20 C in Db/100 mtrs

	ALU-X	ALU6-CR-SAT	ALU6-CS	ALU8000-SAT	D2VRTM	D2VRTM-E-SAT	HQ96-R	HQ96-S	144R-PRO	144S-PRO
50 MHz	5,60 dB	4,55 dB	5,30 dB	4,80 dB	5,60 dB	4,50 dB	4,95 dB	5,08 dB	5,20 dB	5,29 dB
200 MHz	10,50 dB	8,41 dB	10,30 dB	8,20 dB	11,28 dB	8,51 dB	10,50 dB	11,45 dB	10,48 dB	11,50 dB
300 MHz	12,45 dB	10,48 dB	13,30 dB	10,15 dB	14,00 dB	10,44 dB	12,40 dB	15,55 dB	12,93 dB	15,30 dB
500 MHz	16,10 dB	13,10 dB	17,00 dB	13,05 dB	18,55 dB	13,54 dB	16,80 dB	22,72 dB	16,83 dB	21,00 dB
800 MHz	22,50 dB	16,90 dB	21,80 dB	16,70 dB	23,80 dB	17,00 dB	21,90 dB	25,30 dB	20,50 dB	23,20 dB
1000 MHz	25,28 dB	19,28 dB	26,30 dB	19,10 dB	28,00 dB	20,72 dB	24,93 dB	28,00 dB	25,25 dB	27,00 dB
1350 MHz	29,00 dB	23,55 dB		22,00 dB		24,00 dB	32,50 dB		31,13 dB	
1750 MHz	33,00 dB	27,48 dB		26,10 dB		27,20 dB	35,60 dB		34,92 dB	
2050 MHz	36,07 dB	30,07 dB		28,90 dB		29,90 dB	41,80 dB		40,65 dB	
IMPEDENZA NOMINALE / NOMINAL IMPEDANCE	75 Ohm ± 2	75 Ohm ± 2	75 Ohm ± 2	75 Ohm ± 2	75 Ohm ± 2	75 Ohm ± 2	75 Ohm ± 2	75 Ohm ± 2	75 Ohm ± 2	75 Ohm ± 2
VELOCITÀ DI PROPAGAZIONE / VELOCITY RATIO	75%	81%	80%	80%	66%	82%	80%	80%	82%	80%
CAPACITÀ / CAPACITY	56 pF/mt	52 pF/mt	56 pF/mt	52 pF/mt	67 pF/mt	55 pF/mt	55 pF/mt	55 pF/mt	55 pF/mt	55 pF/mt
EFFICIENZA DI SCHERMATURA / SCREENING EFFICIENCY a 525 MHZ	> 80 dB	> 90 dB	> 75 dB	> 80 dB	> 90 dB	> 80 dB	> 40 dB	> 40 dB	> 55 dB	> 60 dB
a 1500 MHZ	> 80 dB	> 80 dB		> 90 dB		> 90 dB	> 38 dB		> 45 dB	

LEGENDA / LEGEND

rr = RAME ROSSO / BARE COPPER
rs = RAME STAGNATO / TINNED COPPER
PE = POLITENE COMPATTO / SOLID POLYTHENE
PEE = POLITENE ESPANSO / FOAM POLYTHENE

AL/PET = NASTRO ALLUMINIO MYLAR / ALUMINIUM + MYLAR TAPE
AL/PET/AL = NASTRO ALLUMINIO MYLAR ALLUMINIO / ALUMINIUM + MYLAR + ALUMINIUM TAPE
CU/PET = NASTRO RAME POLIESTERE / COPPER + POLYESTHER TAPE

TUTTI I COASSIALI A CATALOGO SONO ESEGUIBILI A RICHIESTA NELLE SEGUENTI VERSIONI: / ALL CATALOGUE MODELS CAN BE REALIZED ON DEMAND IN THE FOLLOWING VERSIONS:
- DIELETTRICO IN PE COMPATTO CON CONDUTTORE DA 0,80 mm / SOLID PE DIELECTRIC WITH 0,80 mm INNER CONDUCTOR
- GUAINA H.F. A BASSA EMISSIONE FUMI ALOGENIDRICI / HALOGEN FREE OUTER SHEATH
- GUAINA NON PROPAGANTE L'INCENDIO / LOW SMOKE OUTER SHEATH

* I valori e le caratteristiche elettriche soprariportati sono riscontrati e controllati con apparecchiatura H.P. 8753 C / All the above value are checked and verified with a H.P. 8753 C instrument

SEPTEMBER ◆ CATEGORY WINNER

Francesco Vavassori, Italy

OCTOBER ◆ CATEGORY WINNER

John M. Morris, U.S.A.

PRODUCT ILLUSTRATION

NOVEMBER ◆ CATEGORY WINNER

Klaus Hennig, Germany

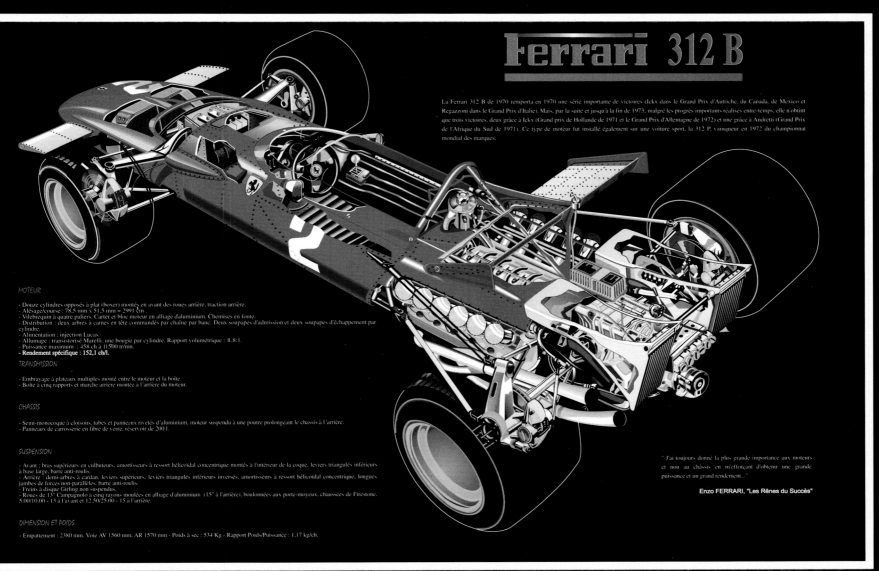

Ferrari 312 B

La Ferrari 312 B de 1970 remporta en 1970 une série importante de victoires (Ickx dans le Grand Prix d'Autriche, du Canada, de Mexico et Regazzoni dans le Grand Prix d'Italie). Mais, par la suite et jusqu'à la fin de 1973, malgré les progrès importants réalisés entre-temps, elle n'obtint que trois victoires, deux grâce à Ickx (Grand prix de Hollande de 1971 et le Grand Prix d'Allemagne de 1972) et une grâce à Andretti (Grand Prix de l'Afrique du Sud de 1971). Ce type de moteur fut installé également sur une voiture sport, la 312 P, vainqueur en 1972 du championnat mondial des marques.

MOTEUR

- Douze cylindres opposés à plat (boxer) montés en avant des roues arrière, traction arrière.
- Alésage/course : 78,5 mm x 51,5 mm = 2991 cm³.
- Vilebrequin à quatre paliers. Carter et bloc moteur en alliage d'aluminium. Chemises en fonte.
- Distribution : deux arbres à cames en tête commandés par chaîne par banc. Deux soupapes d'admission et deux soupapes d'échappement par cylindre.
- Alimentation : injection Lucas.
- Allumage : transistorisé Marelli, une bougie par cylindre. Rapport volumétrique : 11,8:1.
- Puissance maximum : 458 ch à 11500 tr/mn.
- **Rendement spécifique : 152,1 ch/l.**

TRANSMISSION

- Embrayage à plateaux multiples monté entre le moteur et la boîte.
- Boîte à cinq rapports et marche arrière montée à l'arrière du moteur.

CHASSIS

- Semi-monocoque à cloisons, tubes et panneaux rivetés d'aluminium, moteur suspendu à une poutre prolongeant le châssis à l'arrière.
- Panneaux de carrosserie en fibre de verre, réservoir de 200 l.

SUSPENSION

- Avant : bras supérieurs en culbuteurs, amortisseurs à ressort hélicoïdal concentrique montés à l'intérieur de la coque, leviers triangulés inférieurs à base large, barre anti-roulis.
- Arrière : demi-arbres à cardan, leviers supérieurs, leviers triangulés inférieurs inversés, amortisseurs à ressort hélicoïdal concentrique, longues jambes de forces non-parallèles, barre anti-roulis.
- Freins à disque Girling non suspendus.
- Roues de 13" Campagnolo à cinq rayons moulées en alliage d'aluminium (15" à l'arrière), boulonnées aux porte-moyeux, chaussées de Firestone. 5.00/10.00 - 13 à l'avant et 12.50/25.00 - 15 à l'arrière.

DIMENSION ET POIDS

- Empattement : 2380 mm, Voie AV 1560 mm, AR 1570 mm - Poids à sec : 534 Kg - Rapport Poids/Puissance : 1,17 kg/ch.

" J'ai toujours donné la plus grande importance aux moteurs et non au châssis en m'efforçant d'obtenir une grande puissance et un grand rendement..."

Enzo FERRARI, "Les Rênes du Succès"

JANUARY ◆ CATEGORY WINNER

Cedric Bonhommeau, France

The 1957 Chevy

FEBRUARY ◆ CATEGORY WINNER

Michael Bruggeman, U.S.A.

MARCH/APRIL • CATEGORY WINNER

Stefano Maugeri, Italy

DATI TABULARI DELL'A.B.4

PESO TOTALE .....Kg 7.40(
PESO A VUOTO .....Kg 3.84(
CARICO UTILE ....Kg 3.56(
VELOCITA' MASSIMA SU STRADA ...Km/h 78,3(
VELOCITA' MASSIMA FUORI STRADA ...Km/h 3
AUTONOMIA .....Km 400 (h 8
PENDENZA MASSIMA SUPERABILE ...30°
GRADINO MASSIMO SUPERABILE ...mm 30(
PROFONDITA' DI GUADO (senza accessori) ...mm 70(
CONSUMO CARBURANTE PER 100 Km ...LITRI 45
CONSUMO CARBURANTE PER 100 Km (fuori strada) LITRI 37
CAPACITA' DEL SERBATOIO PRINCIPALE ...LITRI 11(
CAPACITA' DEL SERBATOIO DI RISERVA ...LITRI 20+5
CAPACITA' DELLA DOTAZIONE DI OLIO LUBRIFICANTE LITRI 13+5,2+4,8+1
CAPACITA' DELLA DOTAZIONE DI ACQUA REFRIGERANTE LITRI 3:
EQUIPAGGIO .....N°
RADIO RICETRASMITTENTE .....MARELLI 3M-R

CORAZZATURA SCAFO
ANTERIORE .....mm (
LATERALE .....mm (
POSTERIORE .....mm (
CIELO .....mm (
FONDO .....mm (
CORAZZATURA TORRETTA
ANTERIORE .....mm (
LATERALE .....mm (
POSTERIORE .....mm (
CIELO .....mm (

ARMAMENTO
1 CA....O BREDA M35 DA 20mm ...con 456 proiettili in 57 caricatori da (
2 MITRAGLIATRICI BREDA 38 ...con 1992 colpi in 83 caricatori da 2(

MOTORE
CILINDRI .....N°6
ALESAGGIO .....mm 9(
CORSA .....mm 11:
CILINDRATA TOTALE .....cc 499:
RAPPORTO COMPRESSIONE 5,5
REGIME MASSIMO .....g.p.m. 270(
POTENZA MASSIMA .....HP 8(
RAPPORTO PESO/POTENZA .....HP/tonn. 10,
CARBURATORE .....ZENITH 42 T.T.V.F

AB41

M A Y ◆ CATEGORY WINNER

Enrico Tomaselli, Italy

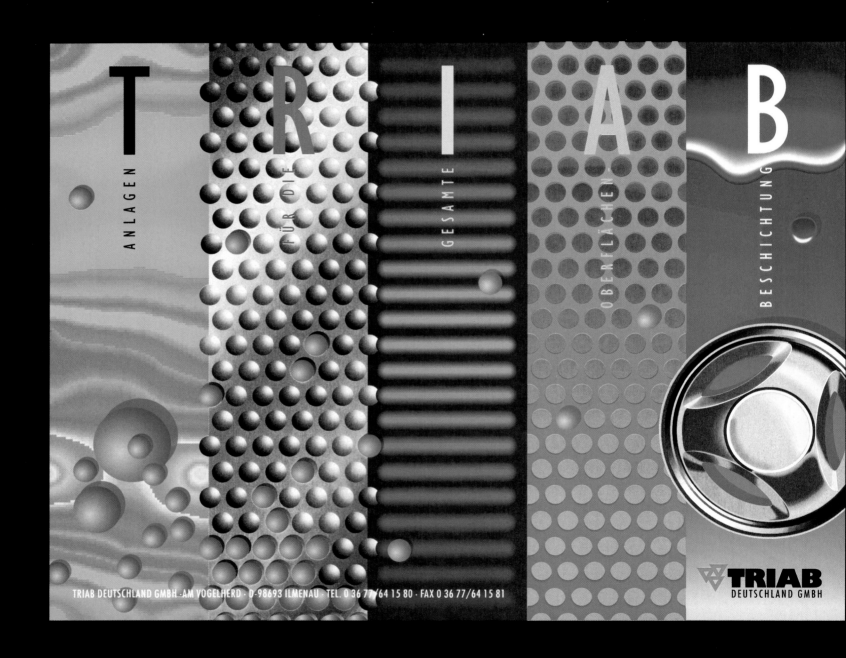

TRIAB

ANLAGEN

FÜR DIE

GESAMTE

OBERFLÄCHEN

BESCHICHTUNG

TRIAB DEUTSCHLAND GMBH · AM VOGELHERD · D-98693 ILMENAU · TEL. 0 36 77/64 15 80 · FAX 0 36 77/64 15 81

TRIAB
DEUTSCHLAND GMBH

OCTOBER ◆ CATEGORY WINNER

Marion Frank/Klaus Hennig, Germany

ENVIRONMENTAL RISK MANAGEMENT

The global environmental revolution is driving future policies and planning. Businesses which adopt positive environmental risk management strategies to lead their management and operations will have the competitive advantage. Municipalities providing drinking water, waste disposal and other services must assure the people that their health and the environment is protected.

AGI K.K. services include:

Environmental audits of practices and operations to assist management with planning

Development of environmental management strategies to prevent, control and clean up pollution

Research of historical operations and possible contamination (Phase I Assessment) to advise property purchasers of environmental risk

Characterization of regional and local geology and hydrogeology to evaluate exposure and risks associated with releases of contamination to the environment

Preliminary investigation of soil and ground-water contamination (Phase II Assessment) to confirm or refute the presence of contamination

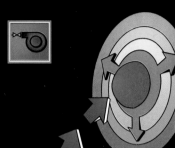

COMPANY ETHICS
CUSTOMER CHOICES

DETAILED EVALUATION

Once contamination of soil and ground water is confirmed, detailed evaluations must be performed to determine the best approach to clean up.

AGI K.K. services include:

Remedial investigations of soil, ground water and contamination to develop a clear understanding of the nature and extent of pollution at and below the ground surface

Fate and transport studies of identified compounds to simulate their future movement and degradation in the solid, liquid or vapor phase or dissolved in ground water

Risk assessments of the threat to people or the environment to establish practical clean up goals which can be demonstrated to be effective

NOVEMBER ◆ CATEGORY WINNER

Jean Lawler, U.S.A.

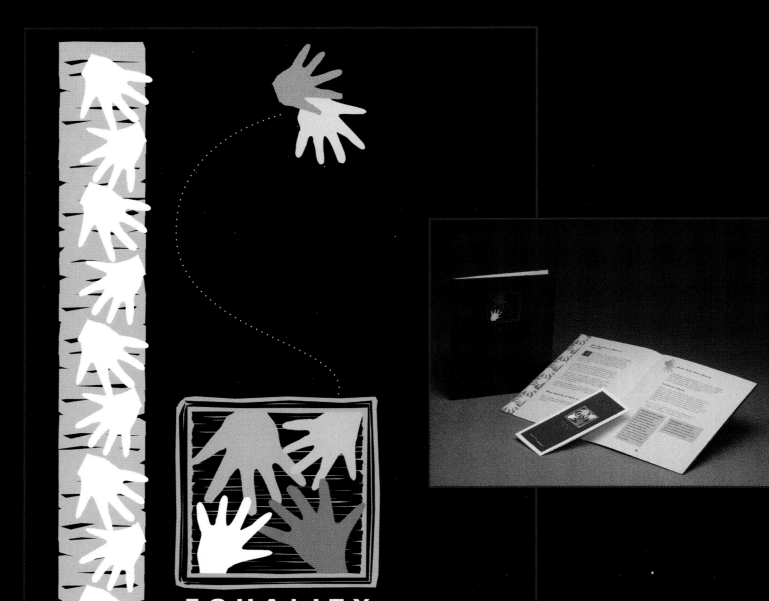

EQUALITY
at WORK

DECEMBER ◆ CATEGORY WINNER

Mary Endress, Canada

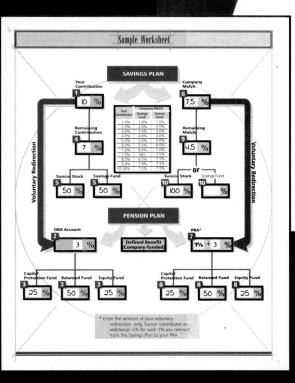

JANUARY ◆ CATEGORY WINNER

Rick Mank, Canada

imaging
PressGraph

Artes Gráficas y Comunicación en la Era Digital - Nº 230 - Febrero 1995 - 750 Ptas.

COLOR PUBLISHING. Copia integral de la imagen
INFOGRAFÍA. La creatividad de las máscaras
MERCADOS Y NEGOCIOS. Mercados de la comunicación, visiones y estrategias
NUEVAS TECNOLOGÍAS. Ver el mundo en 3D
DRUPA' 95. Desafíos y oportunidades

MARCH/APRIL • CATEGORY WINNER

Montserrat Noguera Muntadas, Spain

RANDALL ENTERPRISES

► Creative graphic design services

► Development of corporate materials

► Knowledgeable project coordinators

► Development of marketing/sales strategies

► Ad design/production/media placement

RANDALL ENTERPRISES

MAY ◆ CATEGORY WINNER

Miriam Randall Morrison, U.S.A.

unipro
VALAŠSKÉ MEZIØÍÈÍ

SEPTEMBER ◆ CATEGORY WINNER

Josef Valek/Milan Matous, Czech Republic

OCTOBER ◆ CATEGORY WINNER

Radim Mojzis, Czech Republic

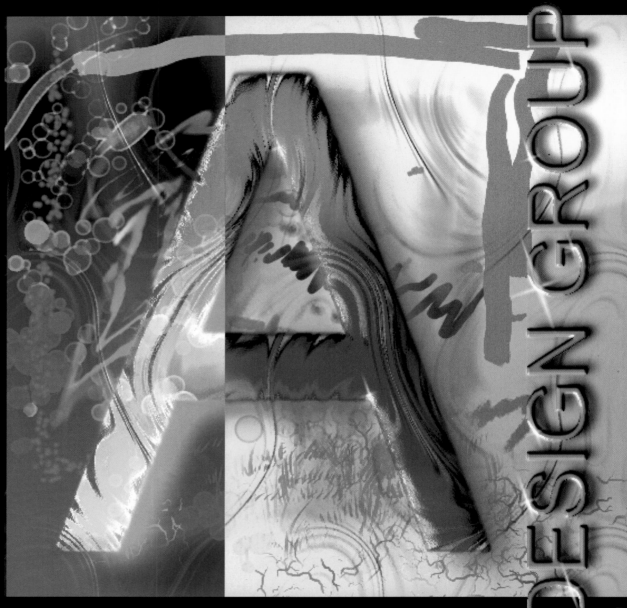

THE COMPUTER DESIGN & ART EXHIBITION

NOVEMBER • CATEGORY WINNER

Piotr Lopatka, Poland

DECEMBER ◆ CATEGORY WINNER

Edward Cristina, Canada

JANUARY ◆ CATEGORY WINNER

Rene Ebert, Germany

FEBRUARY ◆ CATEGORY WINNER

Mike Sturba/Russell Wilson, Canada

Finnegans

Finnegans

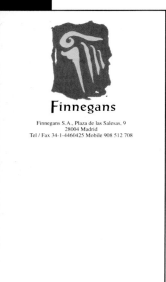

Finnegans

Finnegans S.A., Plaza de las Salesas, 9
28004 Madrid
Tel / Fax 34-1-4460425 Mobile 908 512 708

With Compliments

Finnegans S.A.,

Plaza de las Salesas, 9

28004 Madrid

Tel / Fax 34-1-4460425

Mobile 908 512 708

M A R C H / A P R I L ◆ CATEGORY WINNER

Peter & John Reddy, Ireland

SEPTEMBER ◆ CATEGORY WINNER

Romain Maffei, Switzerland

OCTOBER ◆ CATEGORY WINNER

Radim Mojzis, Czech Republic

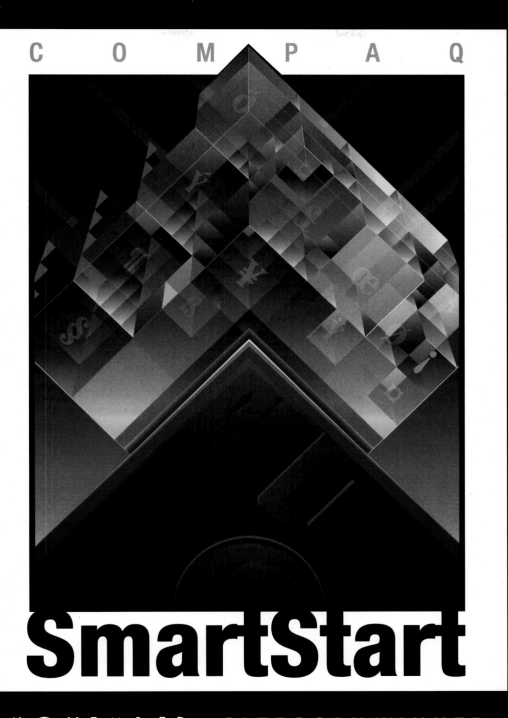

COMPAQ

SmartStart

NOVEMBER ◆ CATEGORY WINNER

Chris Purcell, U.S.A.

"I can drop them off, but you'll have to program them for autoland."

DECEMBER ◆ CATEGORY WINNER

Eric Smith, Canada

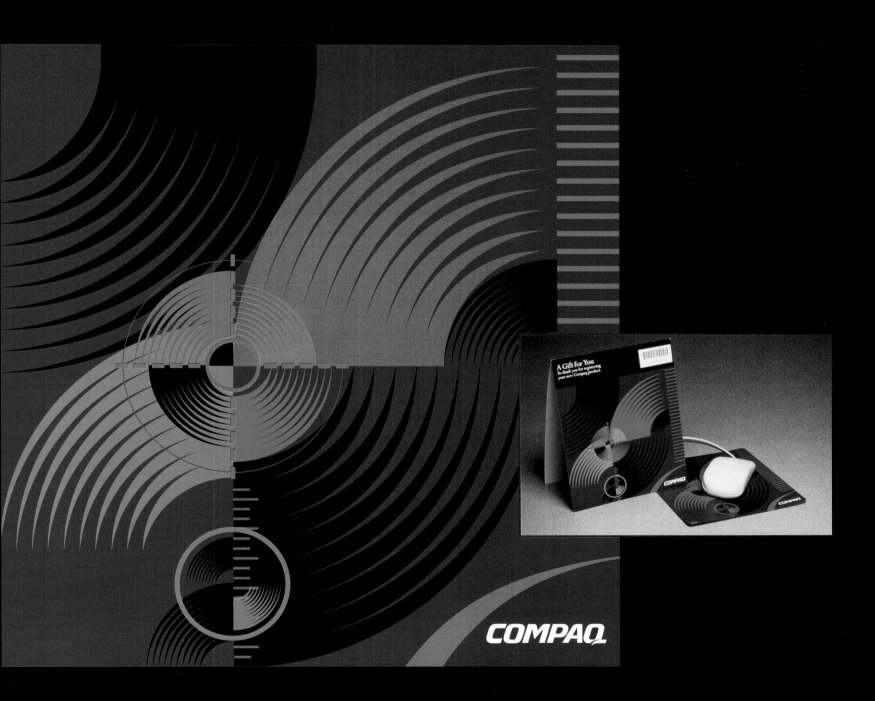

COMPAQ

FEBRUARY ◆ CATEGORY WINNER

Chris Purcell, U.S.A.

CONTENTS:
• Gameboard
• 4 Decks of Cards
• Instructions
• Markers

S·P·O·T·S
NORTH AMERICAN EDITION

AGES: Teen through adult
NUMBER OF PLAYERS: 2-4 or teams
PLAYING TIME: 1 Hour
VERSION: 1

MARCH/APRIL ◆ CATEGORY WINNER

Rick Mank, Canada

MAY • CATEGORY WINNER

Filho Salomao, Brazil

Wil Dawson, U.S.A.

Huan Le Tran, Canada

Tibirica Altamiro Dias, Brazil

Jerry Brown, U.S.A.

James-Michael G. Harlan, U.S.A.

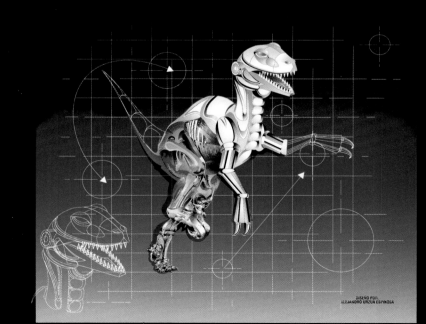

DISEÑO POR:
ALEJANDRO URZUA ESPINOSA

Radim Mojzis, Czech Republic

Lie Tjeng Kian, Indonesia

Amedeo Gigli, Italy

Dalia Levin, Israel

Horst Haas, Germany

Alain Marchand, France

Robert Boutin, Canada

Georgina Curry, U.S.A.

Best of Show 1992

Bill Frymire, Canada

Steve Lyons, U.S.A.

David Brickley, U.S.A.

PEOPLE, PLANTS AND ANIMALS

★1 ★2 ★3 ★4 ★5 ★6

★7 ★8 ★9 ★10 ★11 ★12

★13 ★14 ★15 ★16 ★17 ★18

★19 ★20 ★21 ★22 ★23 ★24

★25 ★26 ★27 ★28 ★29 ★30

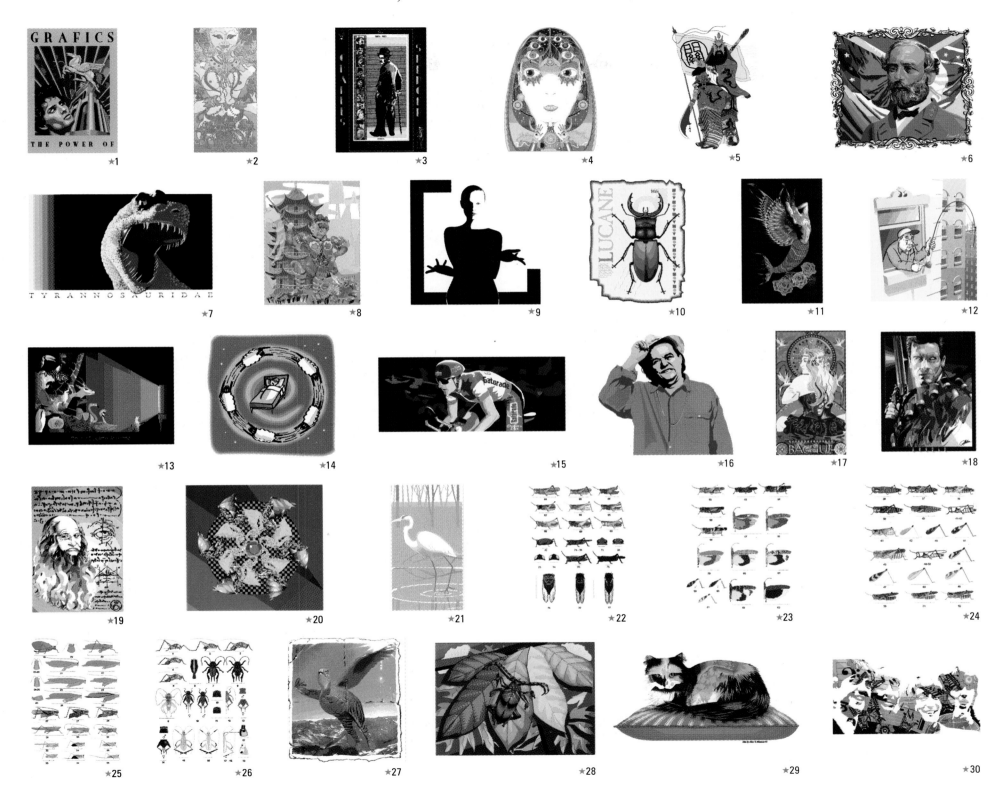

★1 ★2 ★3 ★4 ★5 ★6
★7 ★8 ★9 ★10 ★11 ★12
★13 ★14 ★15 ★16 ★17 ★18
★19 ★20 ★21 ★22 ★23 ★24
★25 ★26 ★27 ★28 ★29 ★30

★1 ★2 ★3 ★4 ★5 ★6
★7 ★8 ★9 ★10 ★11 ★12
★13 ★14 ★15 ★16 ★17 ★18
★19 ★20 21 22 23 24
25 26 27 28 29 30

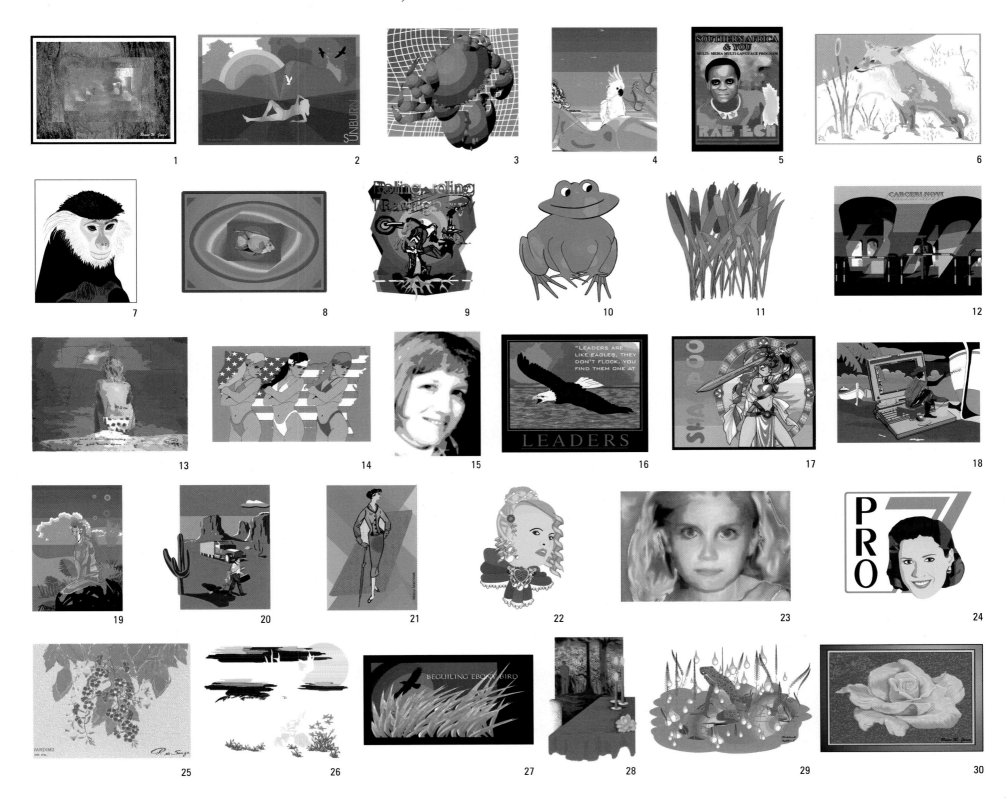

PEOPLE, PLANTS AND ANIMALS

PEOPLE, PLANTS AND ANIMALS

PEOPLE, PLANTS AND ANIMALS

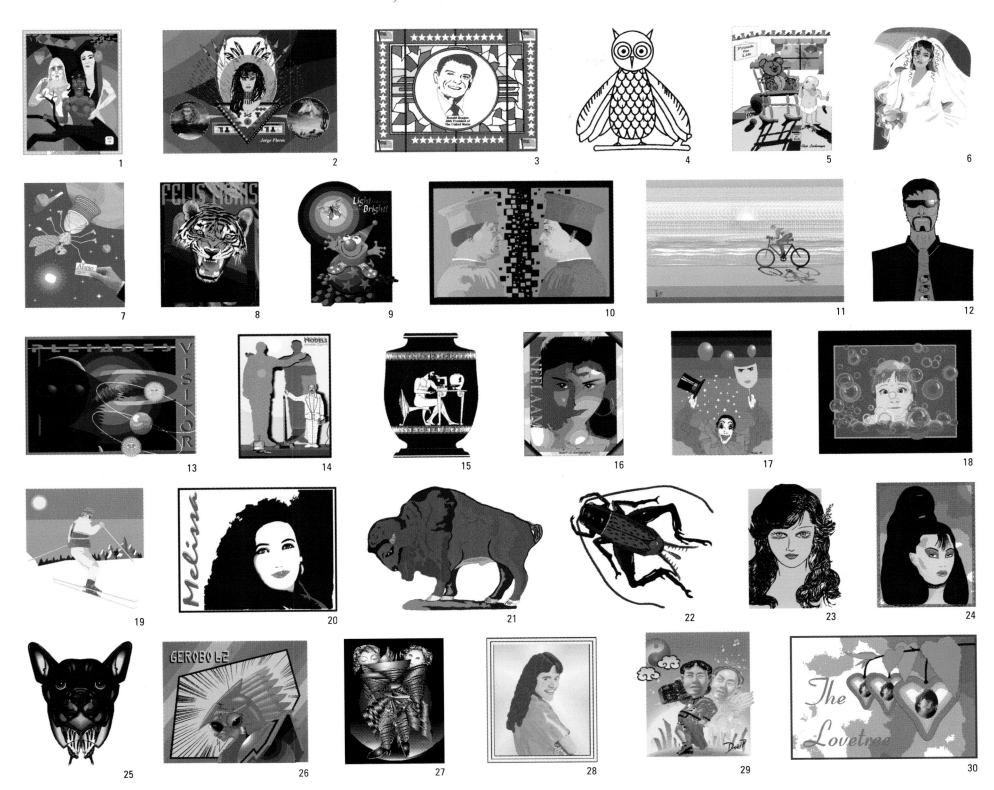

PEOPLE, PLANTS AND ANIMALS

1

2 The Butterfly Series

3

4

5

6

7

8

9

10 Baumfrösche — Australischer Goldlaubfrosch (Hyla aurea)

11

12

13

14

15

16

17

18

19

20

21

22

23

24

25

26

27

28

29

30

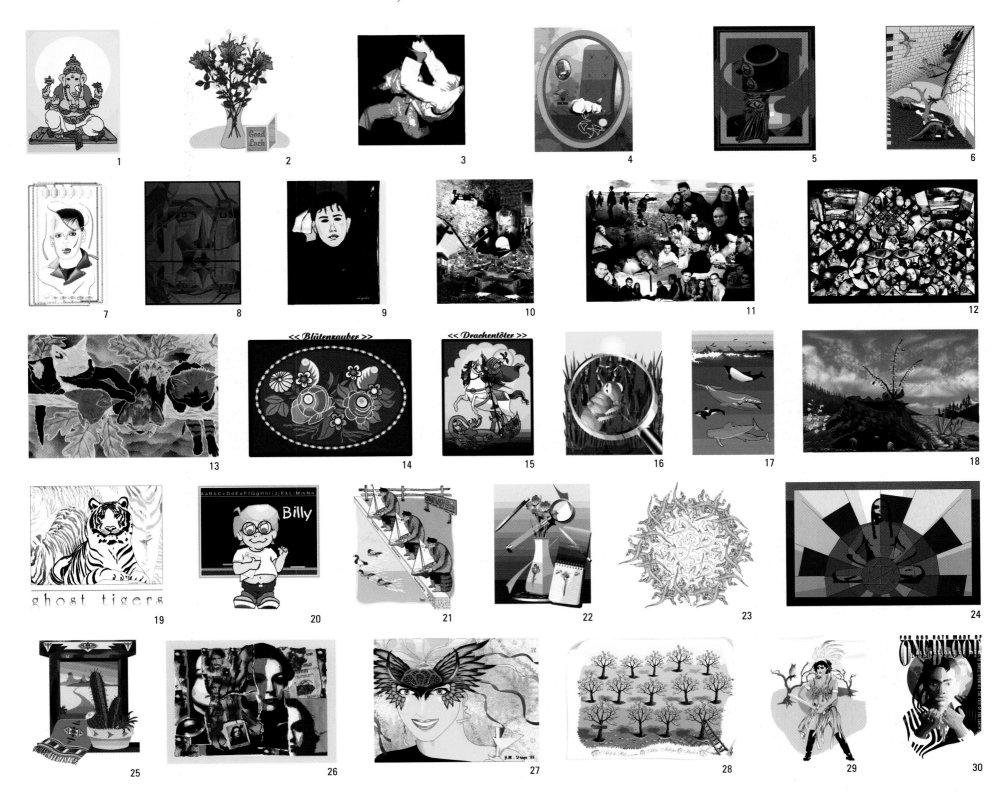

1

2

3

4

5

6

7

8

9

10

11

12

<< Blütenzauber >>

<< Drachentöter >>

13

14

15

16

17

18

ghost tigers

19

Billy

20

21

22

23

24

25

26

27

28

29

30

1
2
3
4
5
6
7
8
9
10
11
12
13
14
15
16
17
18
19
20
21
22
23
24
25
26
27
28
29
30

PEOPLE, PLANTS AND ANIMALS

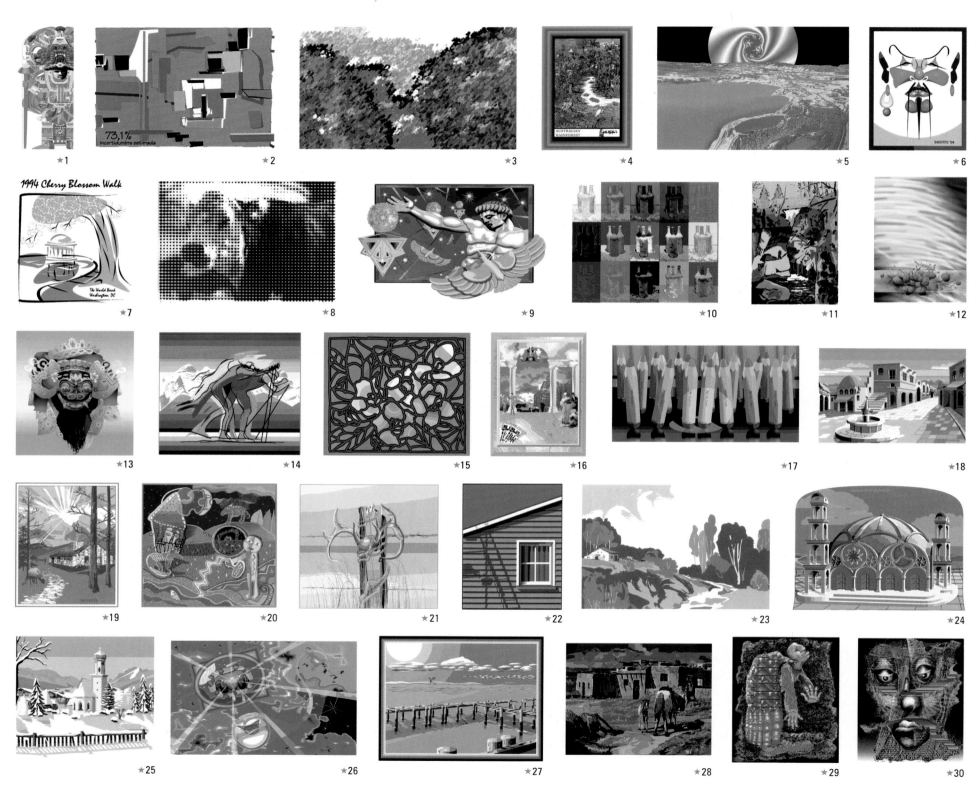

★1 ★2 ★3 ★4 ★5 ★6

★7 ★8 ★9 ★10 ★11 ★12

★13 ★14 ★15 ★16 ★17 ★18

★19 ★20 ★21 ★22 ★23 ★24

★25 ★26 ★27 ★28 ★29 ★30

★1   ★2   ★3   ★4   ★5   ★6
★7   ★8   ★9   ★10   ★11   ★12
★13   ★14   ★15   ★16   ★17   ★18
★19   ★20   ★21   ★22   ★23   ★24
★25   ★26   ★27   ★28   ★29   ★30

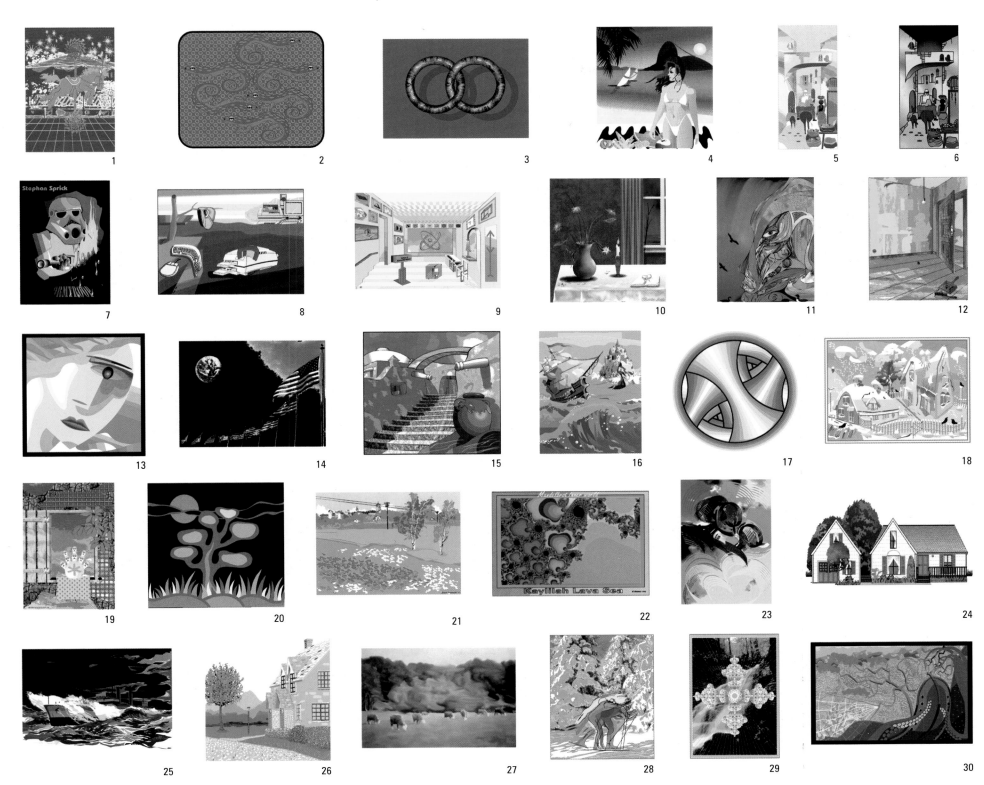

1

2

3

4

5

6

7

8

9

10

11

12

13

14

15

16

17

18

19

20

21

22

23

24

25

26

27

28

29

30

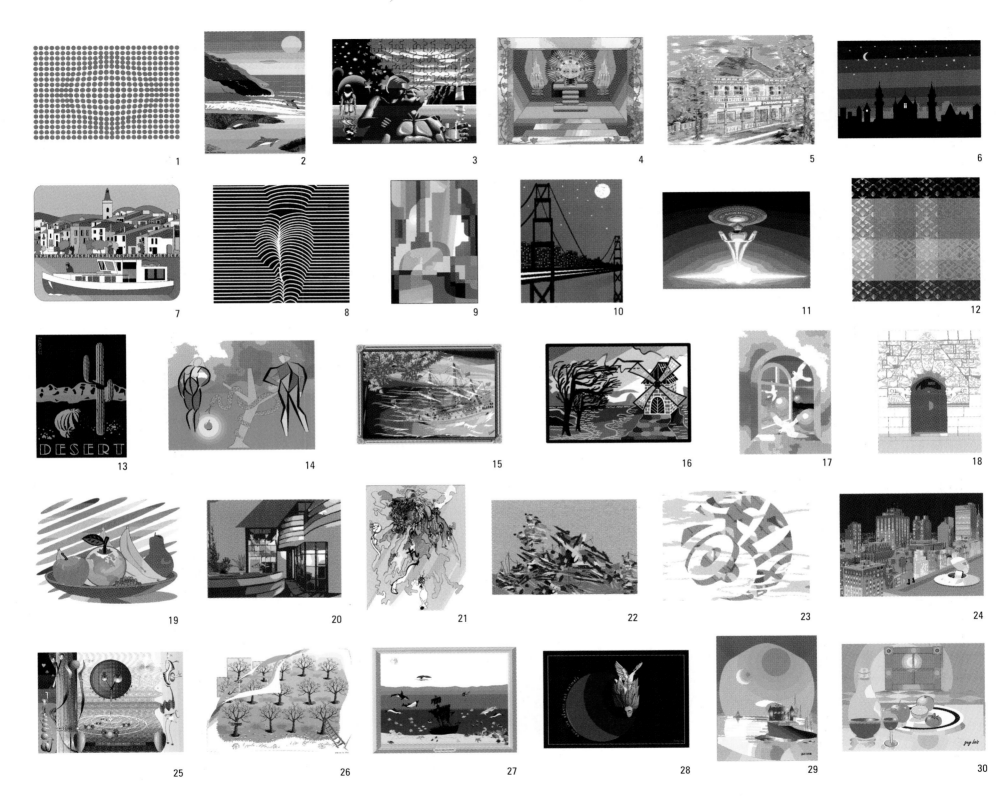

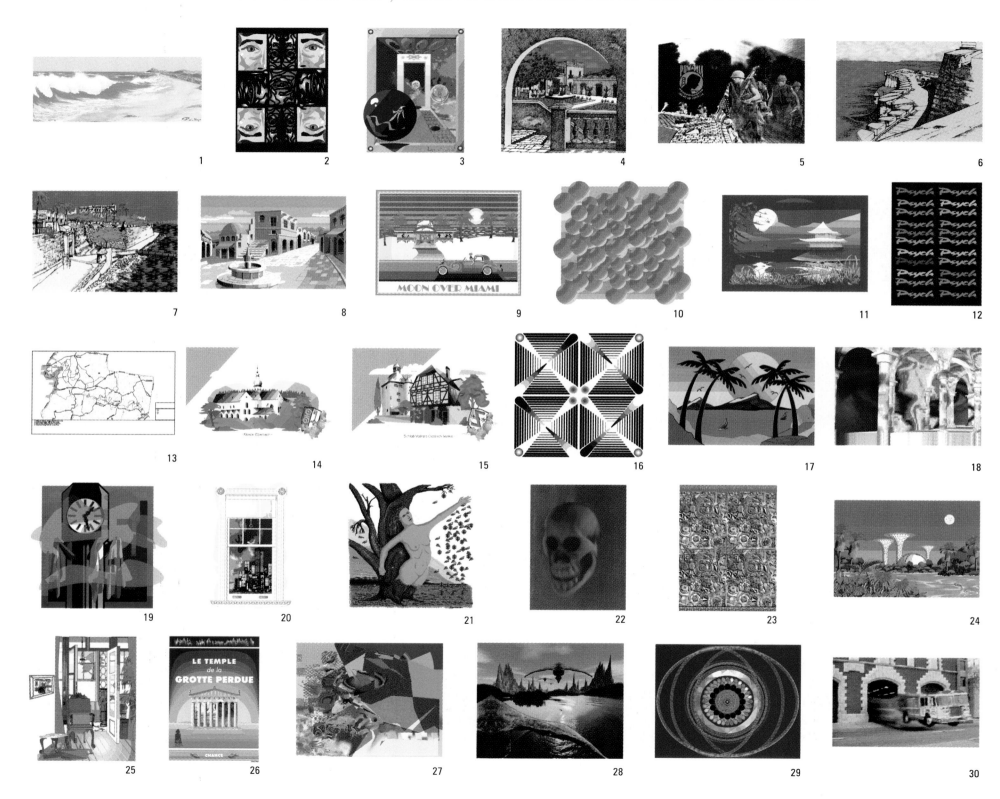

1

2

3

4

5

6

7

8

9

10

11

12

13

14

15

16

17

18

19

20

21

22

23

24

25

26

27

28

29

30

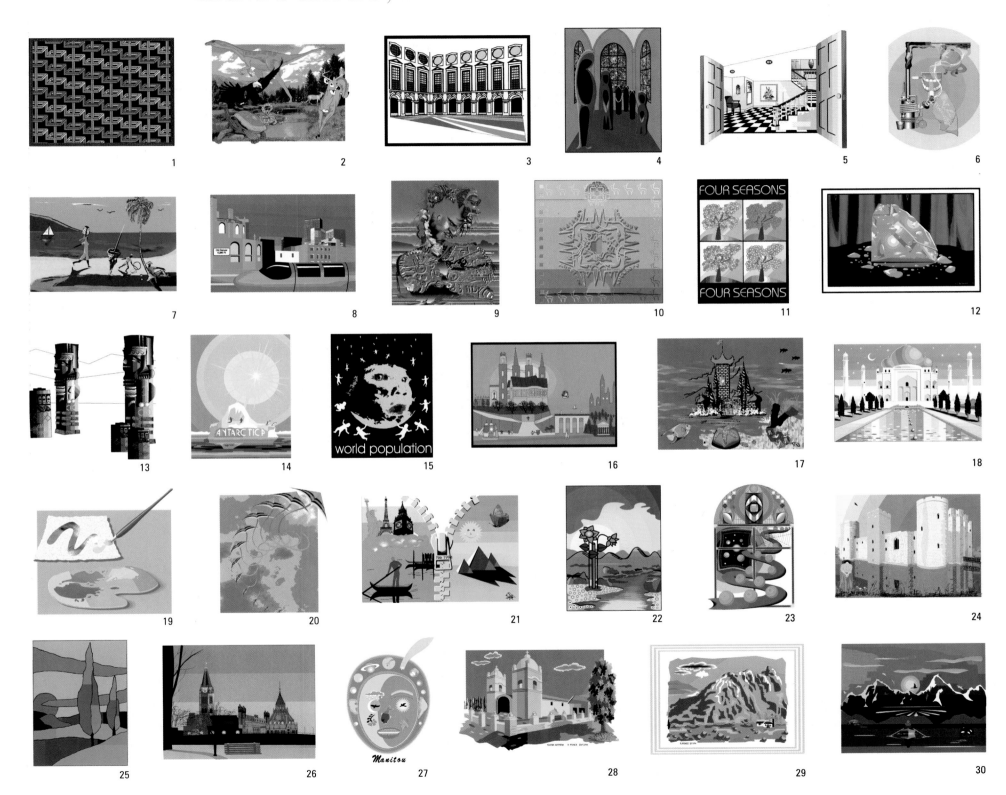

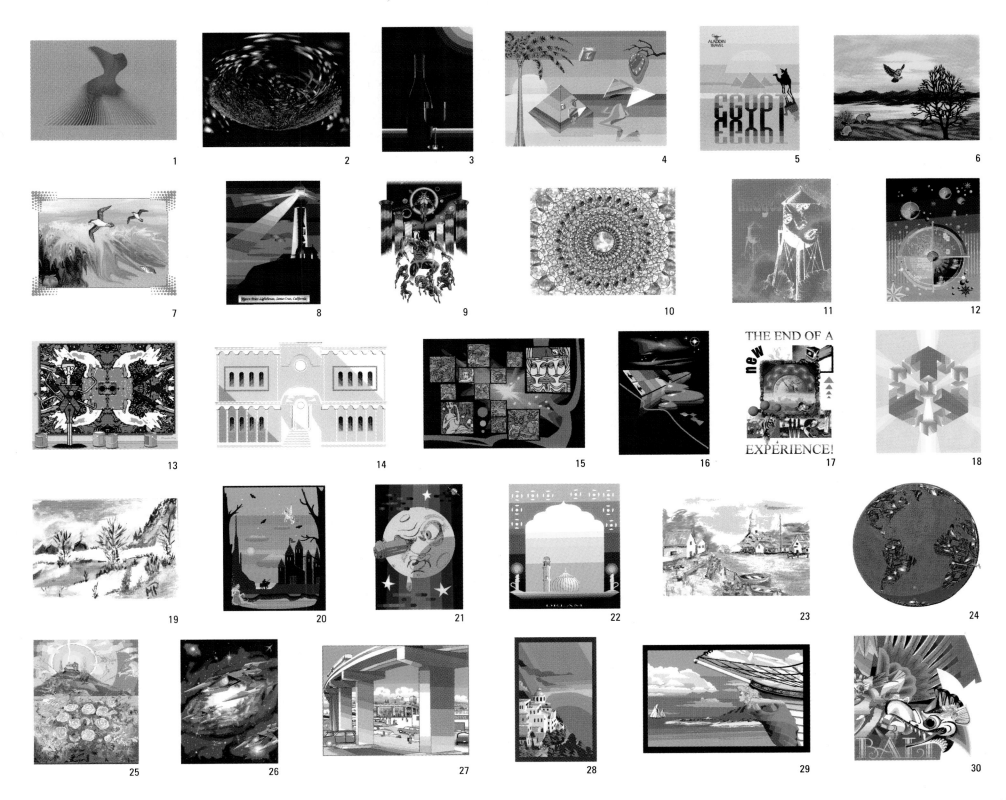

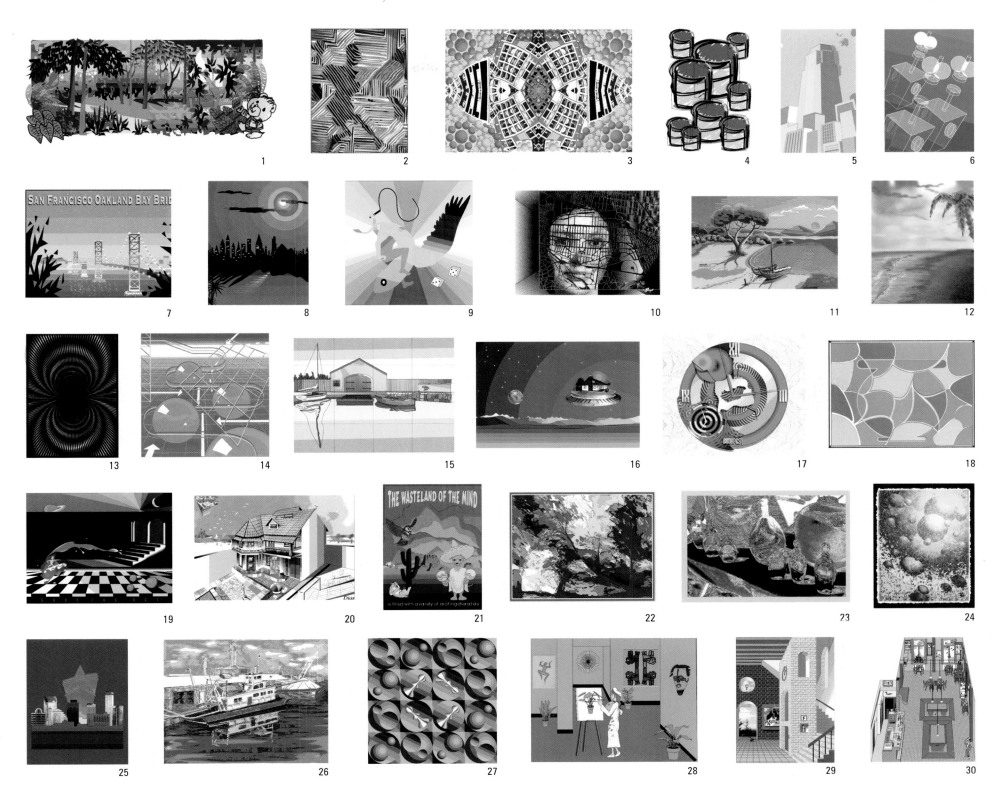

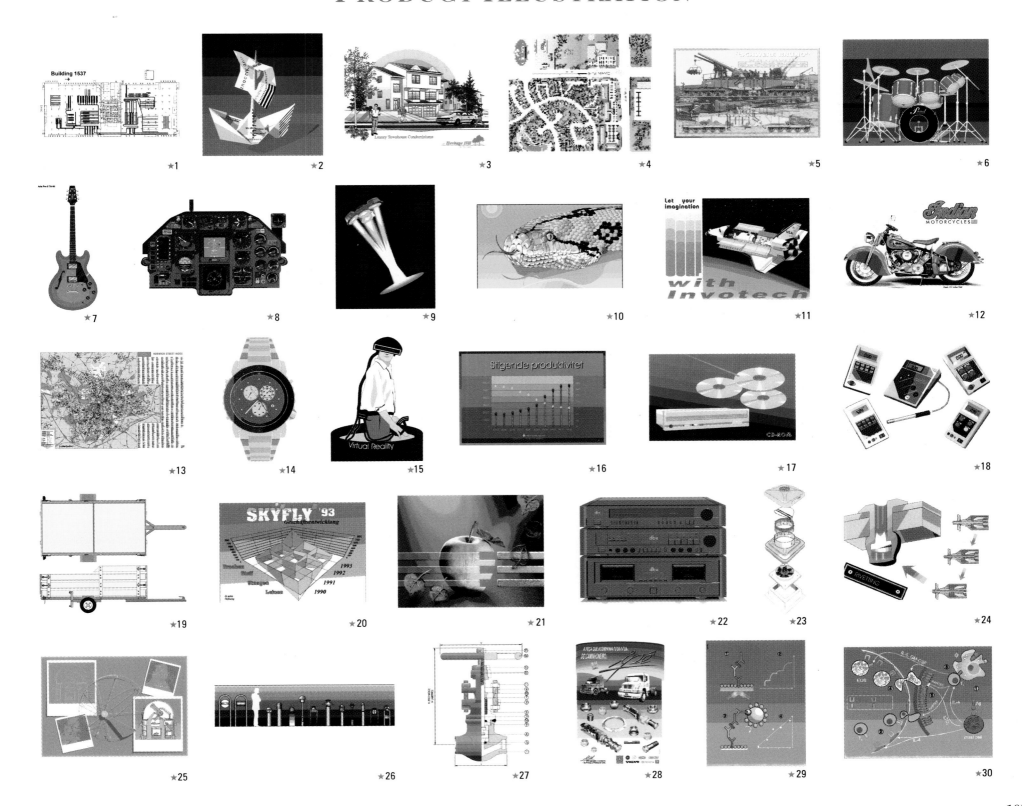

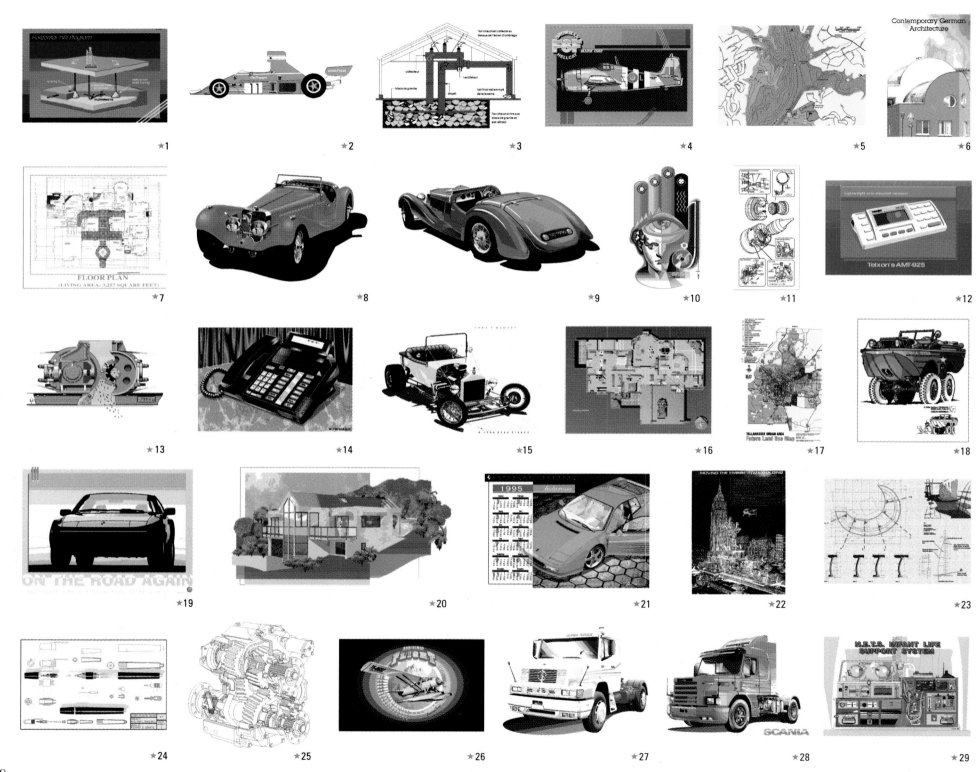

★1 ★2 ★3 ★4 ★5 ★6
★7 ★8 ★9 ★10 ★11 ★12
★13 ★14 ★15 ★16 ★17 ★18
★19 ★20 ★21 ★22 ★23
★24 ★25 ★26 ★27 ★28 ★29

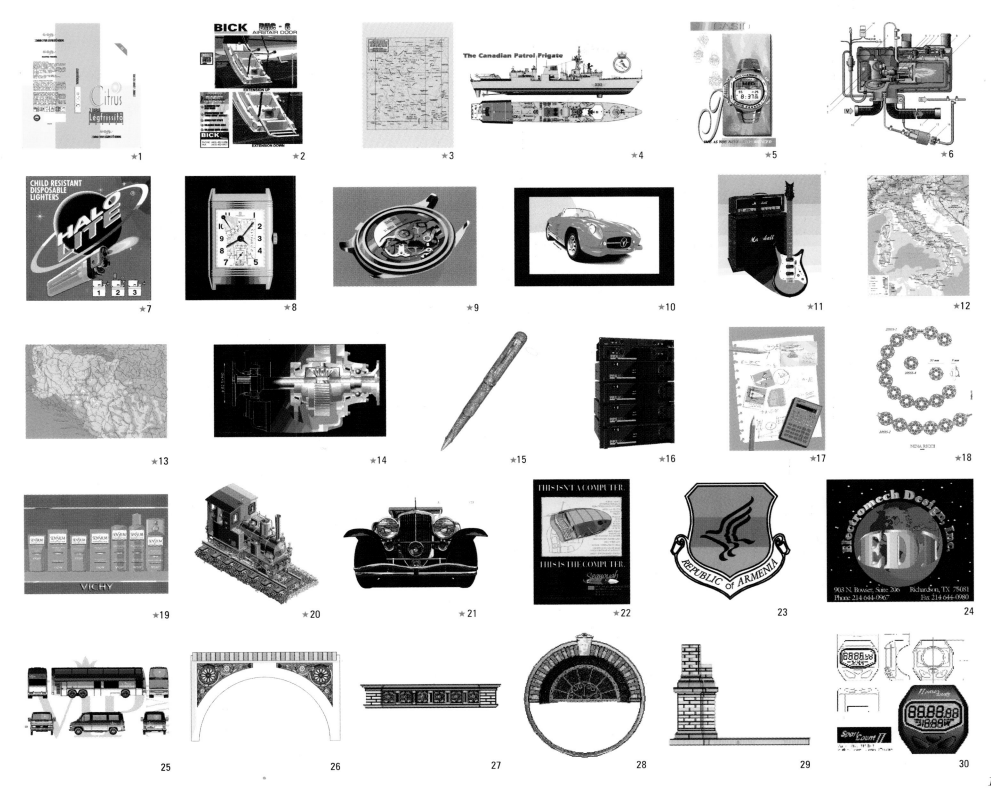

★1   ★2   ★3   ★4   ★5   ★6

★7   ★8   ★9   ★10   ★11   ★12

★13   ★14   ★15   ★16   ★17   ★18

★19   ★20   ★21   ★22   23   24

25   26   27   28   29   30

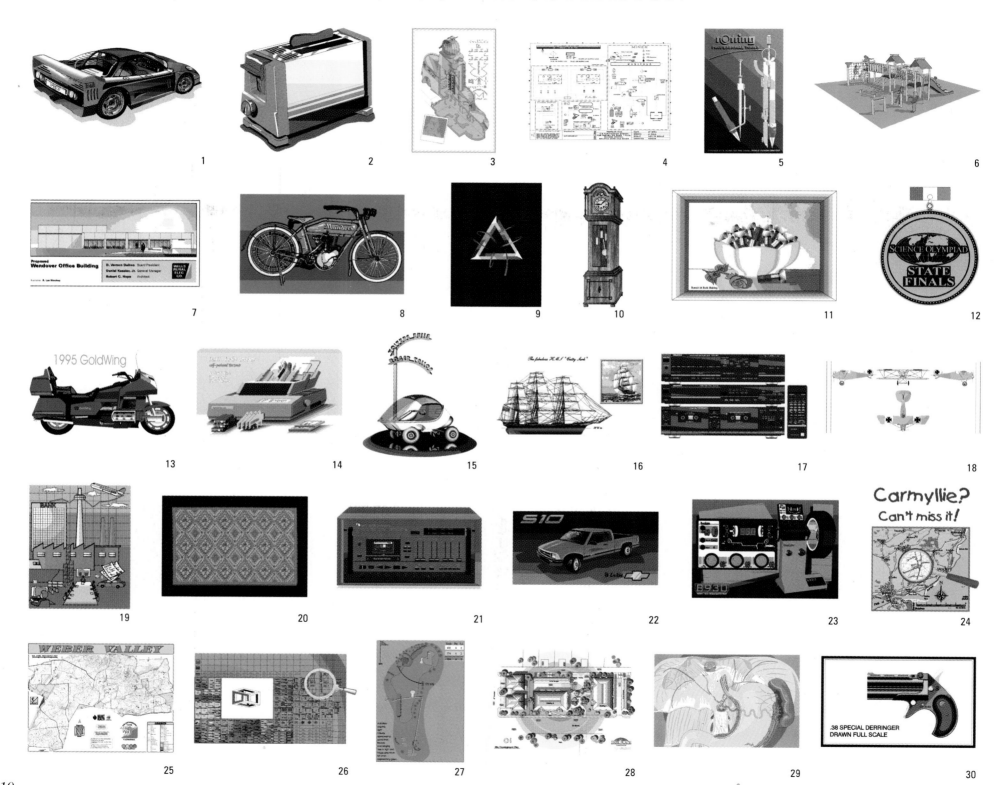

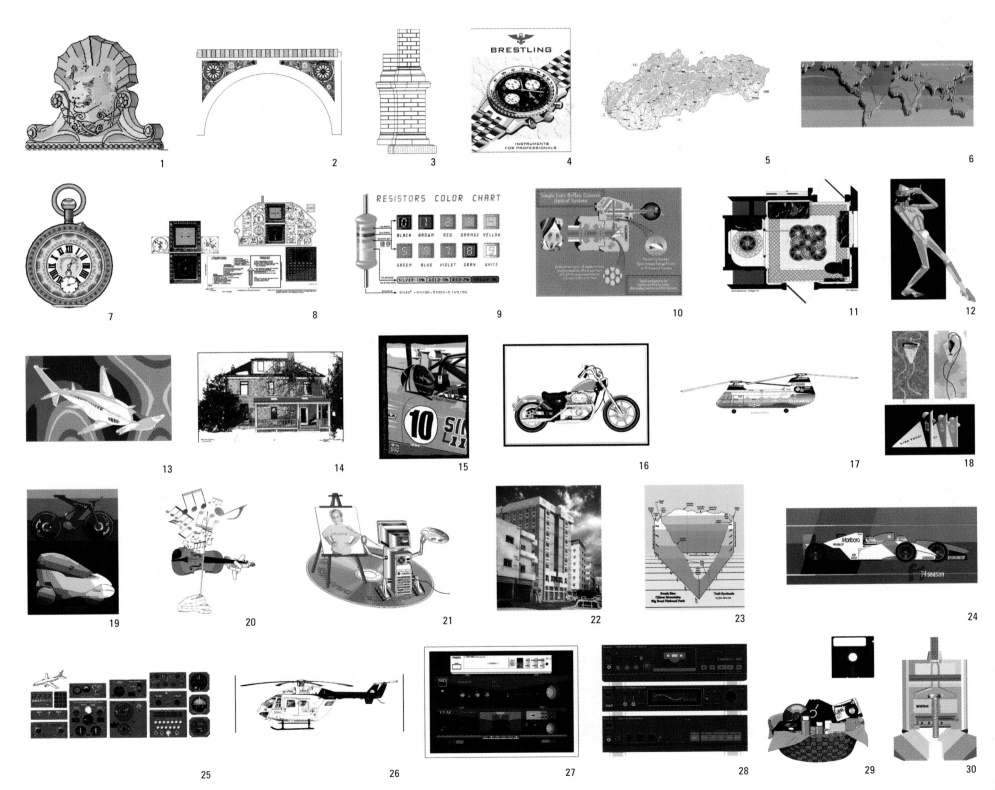

1

2

3

4

5

6

7

8

9

10

11

12

13

14

15

16

17

18

19

20

21

22

23

24

25

26

27

28

29

30

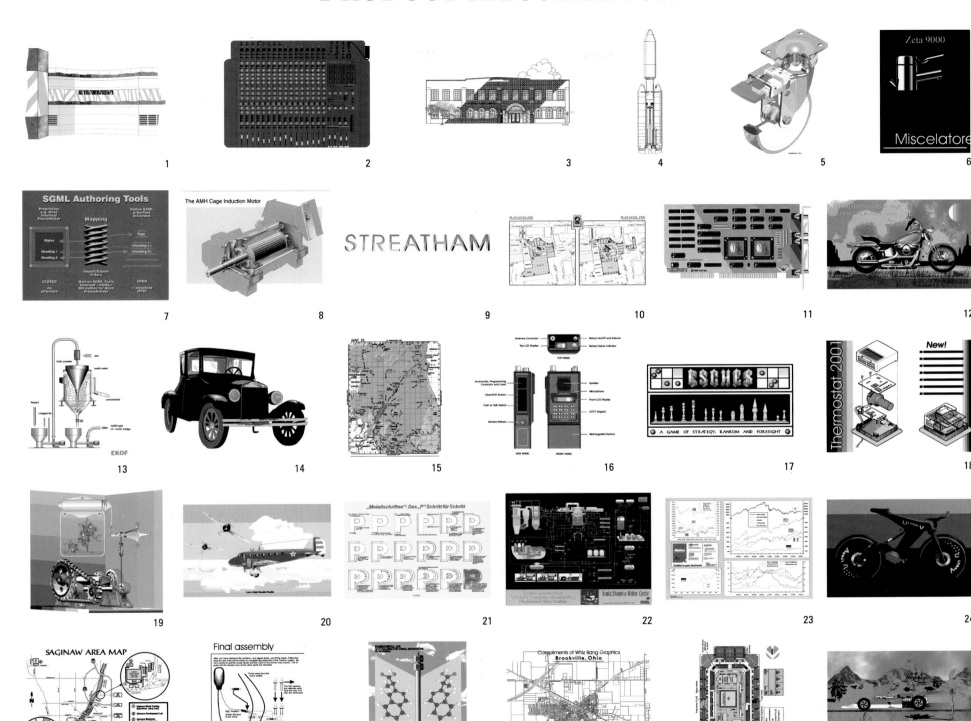

PRODUCT ILLUSTRATION

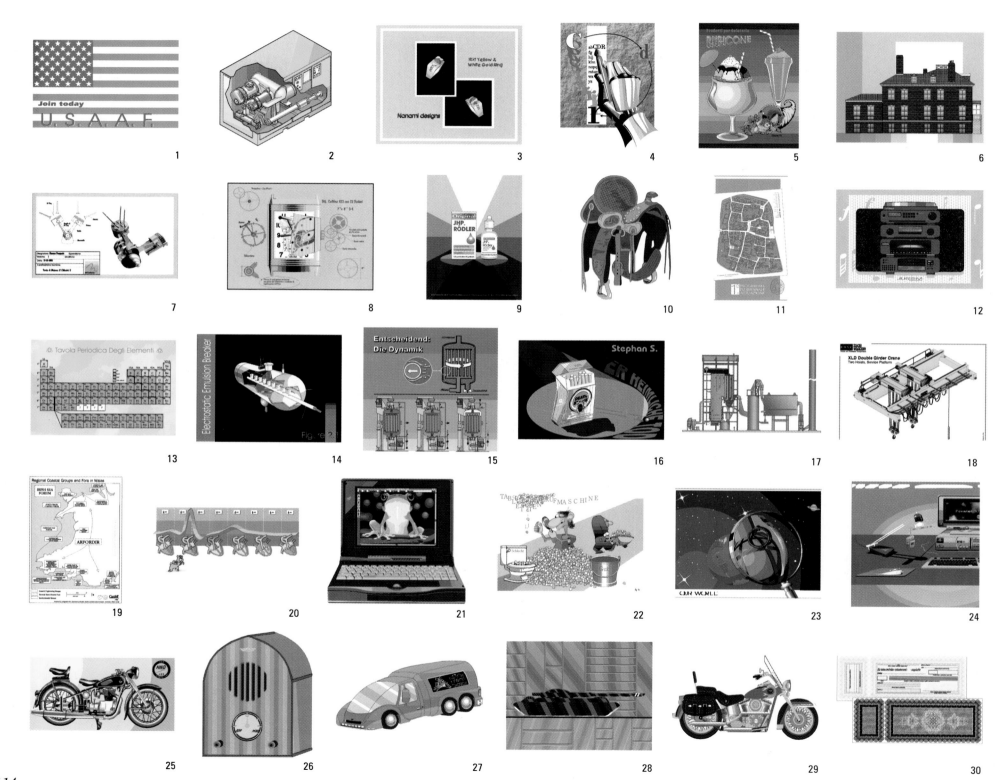

1

2

3

4

5

6

7

8

9

10

11

12

13

14

15

16

17

18

19

20

21

22

23

24

25

26

27

28

29

30

PRODUCT ILLUSTRATION

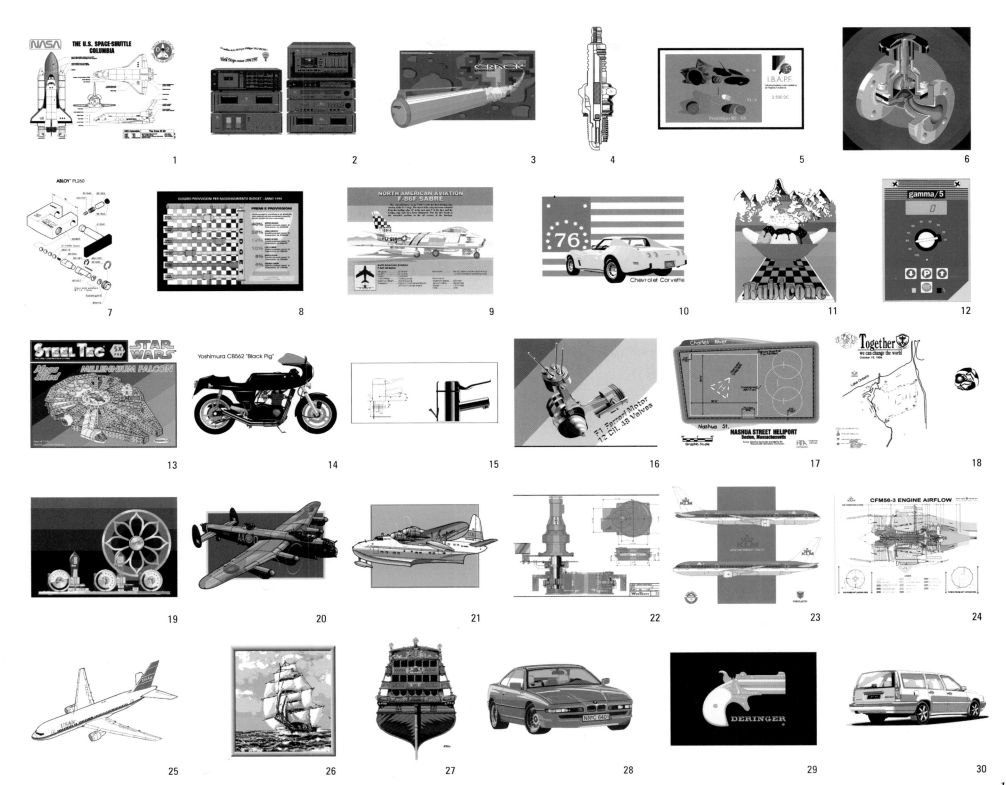

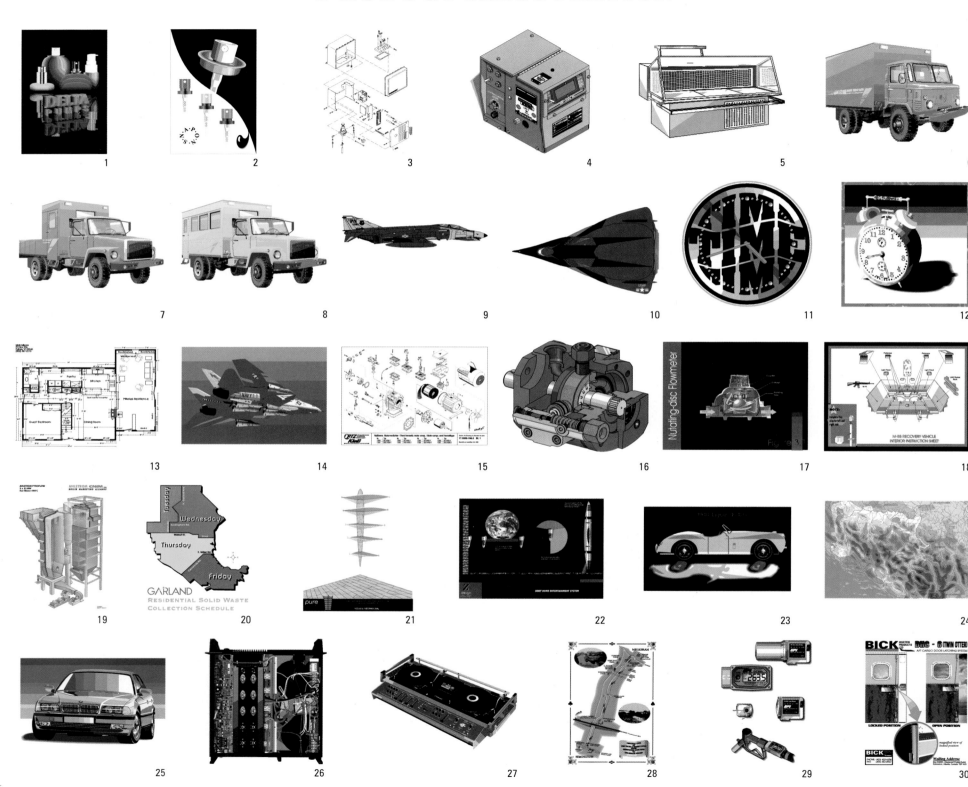

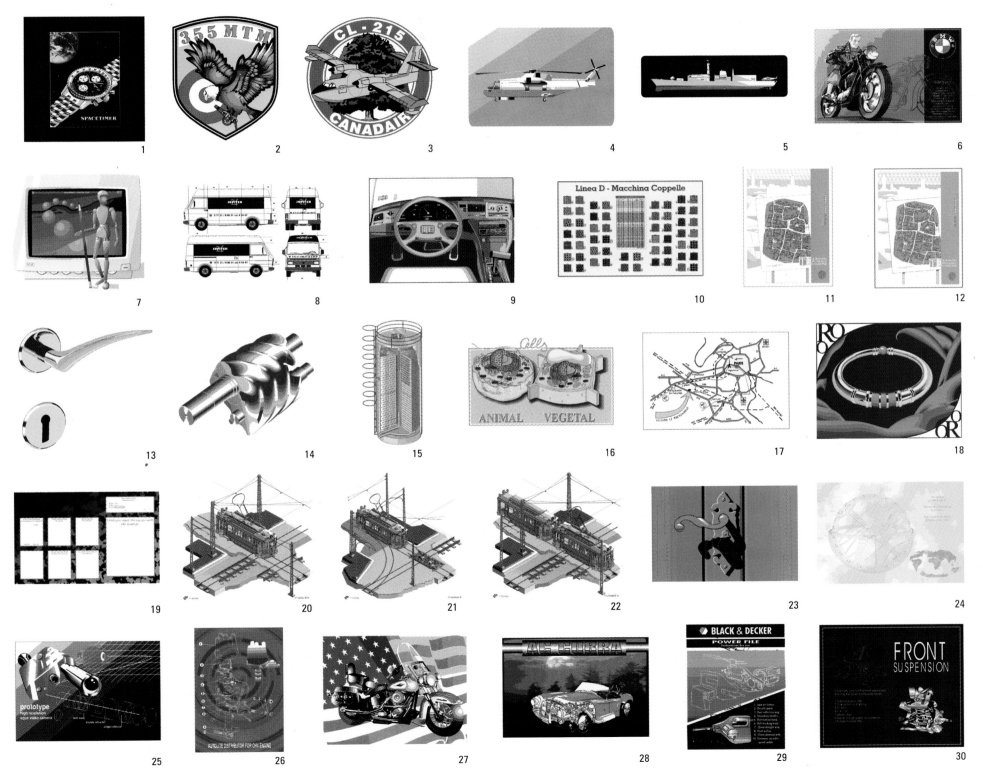

PRODUCT ILLUSTRATION

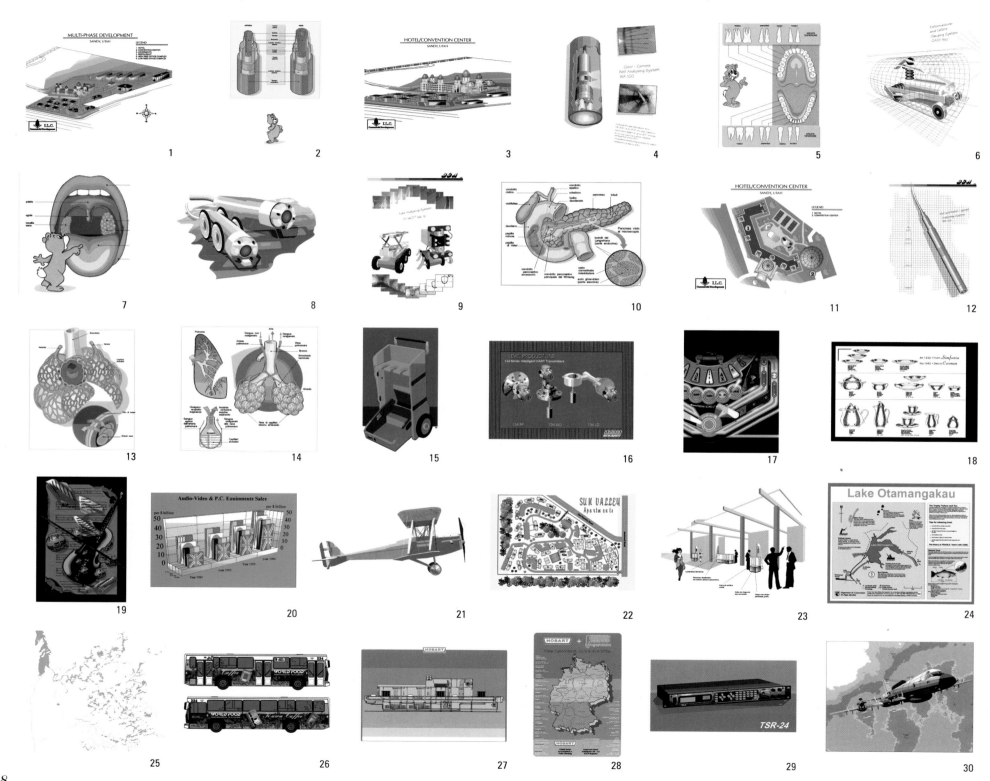

PRODUCT ILLUSTRATION

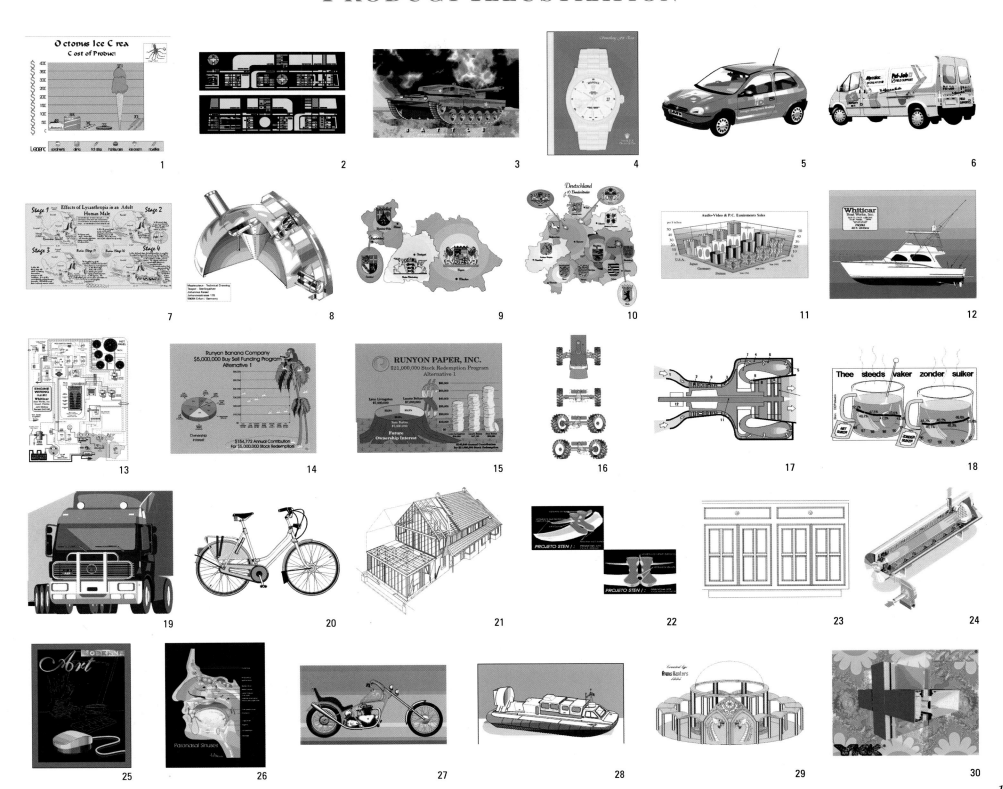

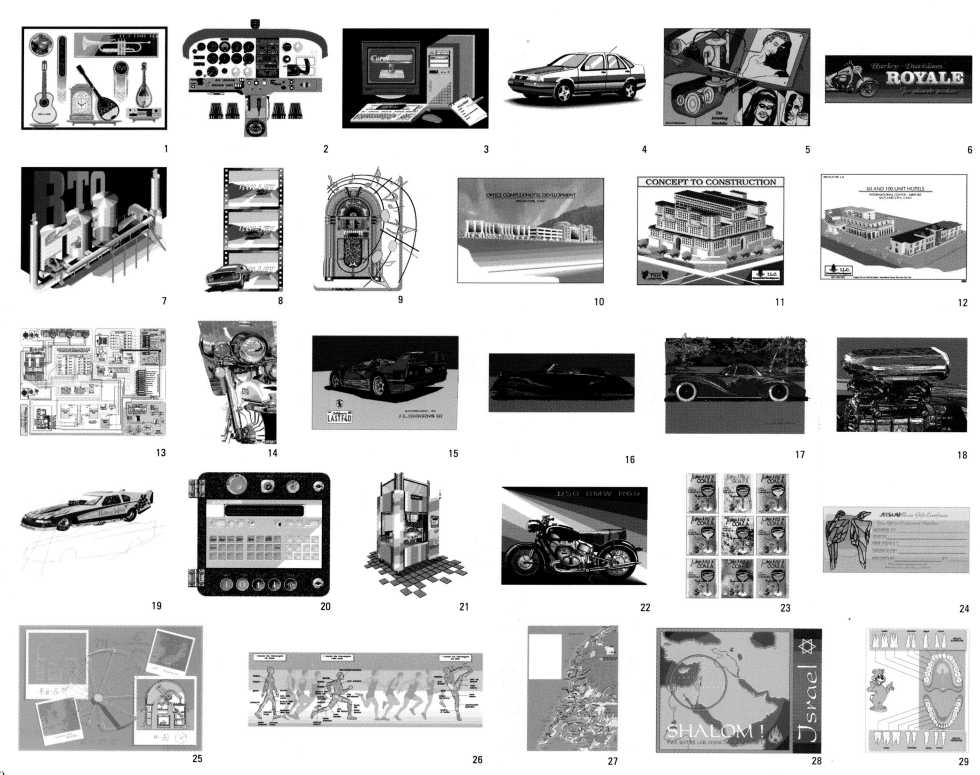

★1 ★2 ★3 ★4 ★5 ★6
★7 ★8 ★9 ★10 ★11 ★12
★13 ★14 ★15 ★16 ★17 ★18
★19 ★20 ★21 ★22 ★23 ★24
★25 ★26 ★27 ★28 ★29 ★30

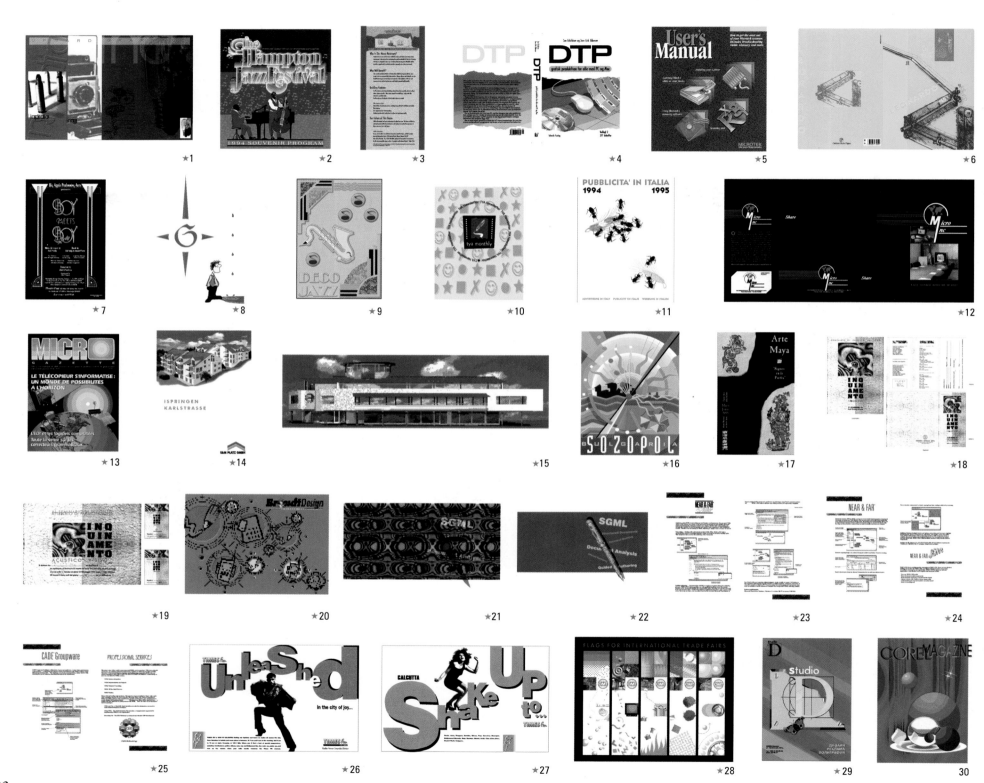

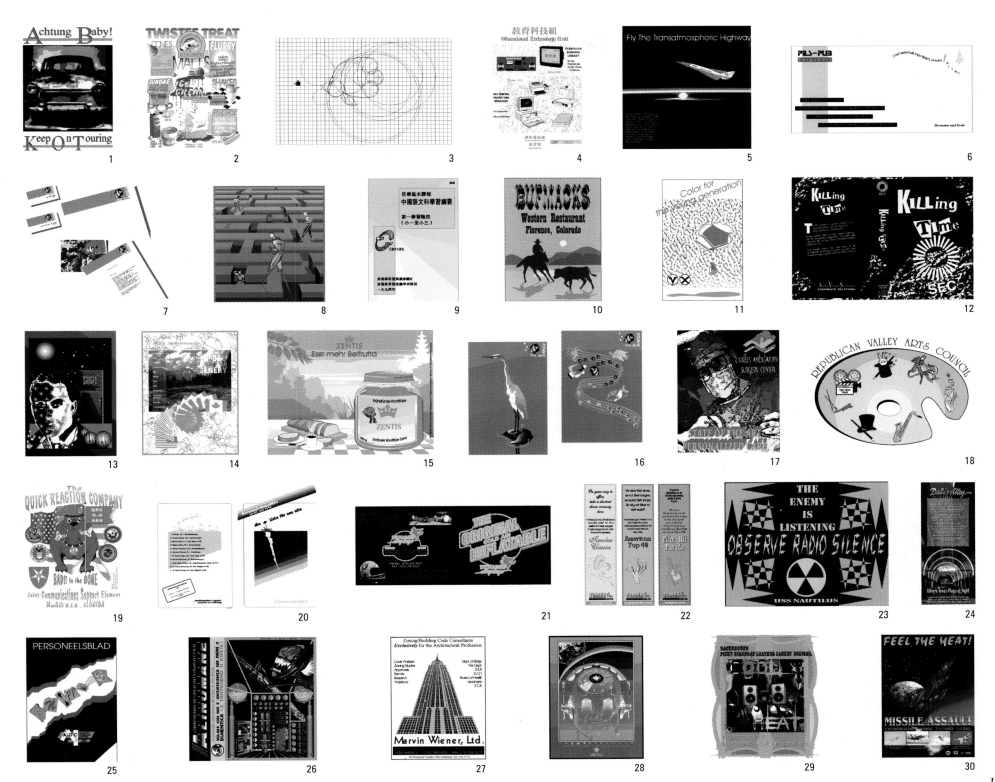

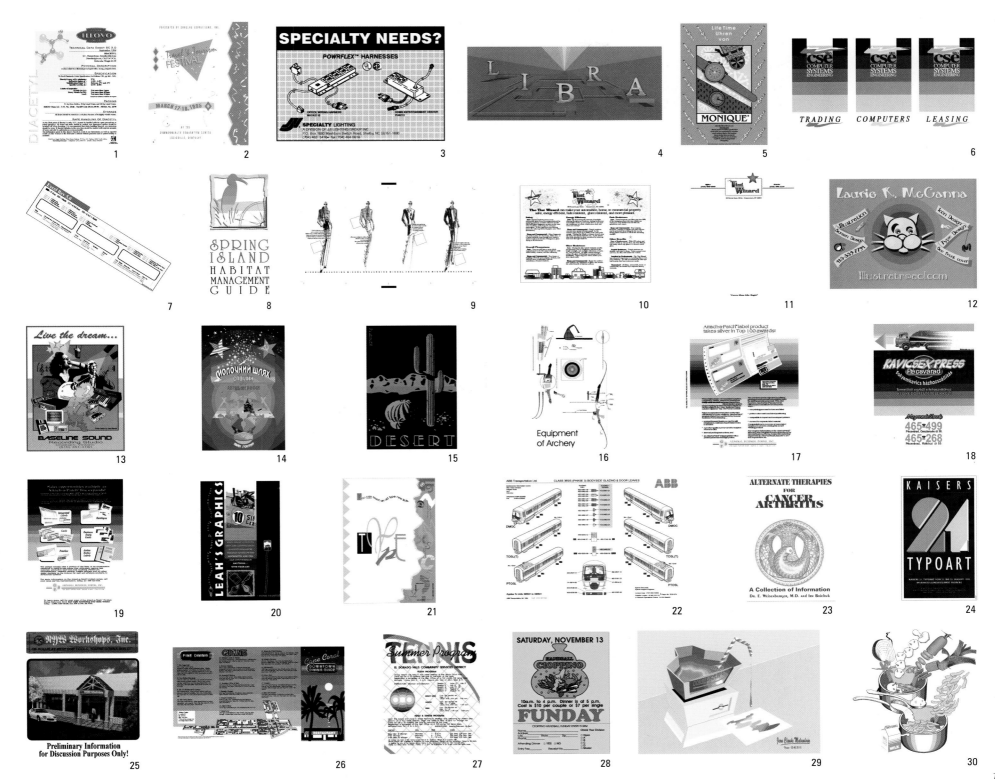

PAGE LAYOUT AND DESIGN

PAGE LAYOUT AND DESIGN

1

TEXAS LOTTERY LAMPOON

2

HOW TO HONESTLY SAY, "KISS ME - I'M RICH"

TEXAS LOTTERY LAMPOON

3

4

5

6

7

8

9

10

11

12

13

14

15

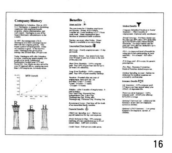

16

17

18

19

20

21

22

23

24

25

26

27

28

29

30

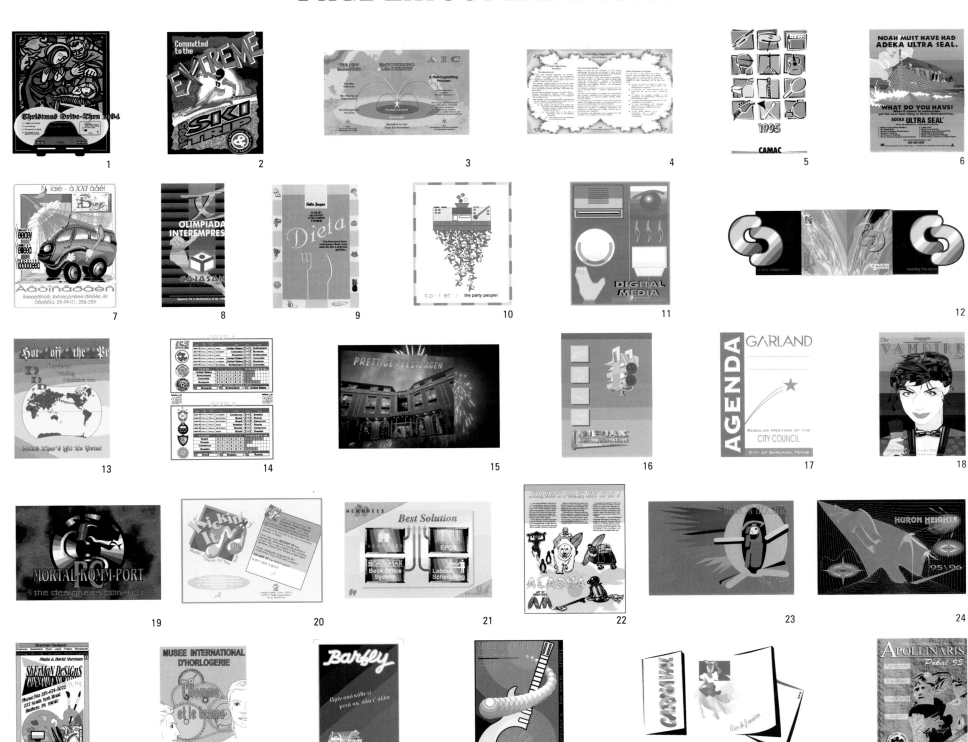

PAGE LAYOUT AND DESIGN

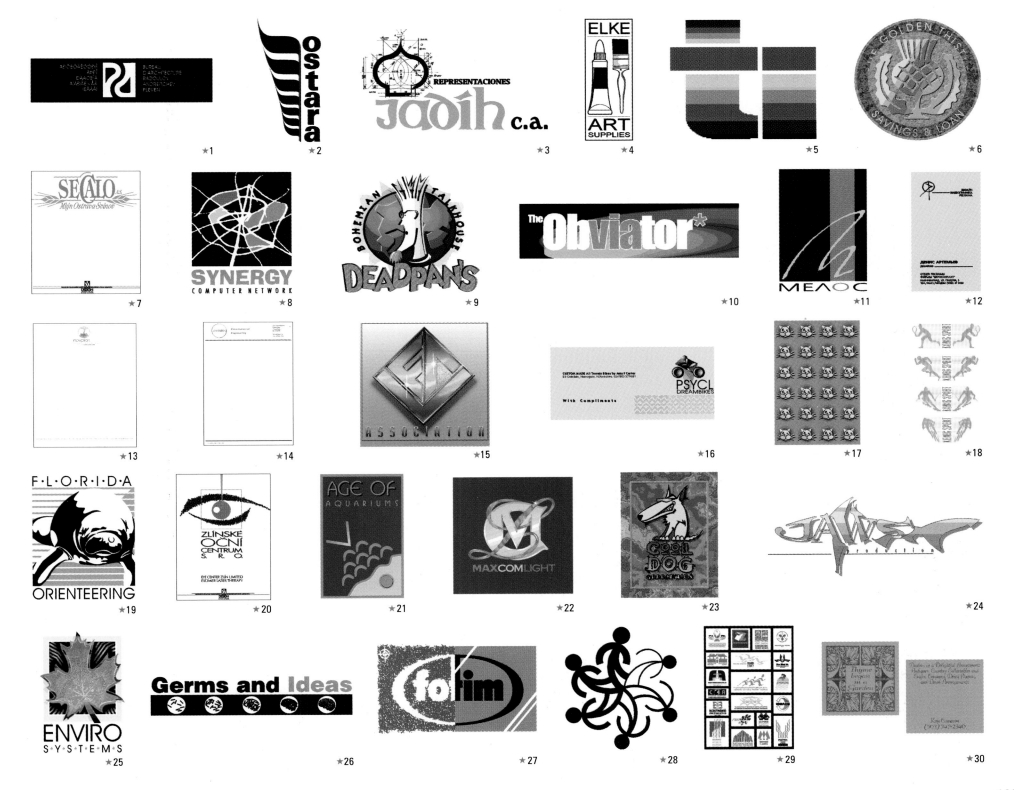

★1 ★2 ★3 ★4 ★5 ★6

★7 ★8 ★9 ★10 ★11 ★12

★13 ★14 ★15 ★16 ★17 ★18

★19 ★20 ★21 ★22 ★23 ★24

★25 ★26 ★27 ★28 ★29 ★30

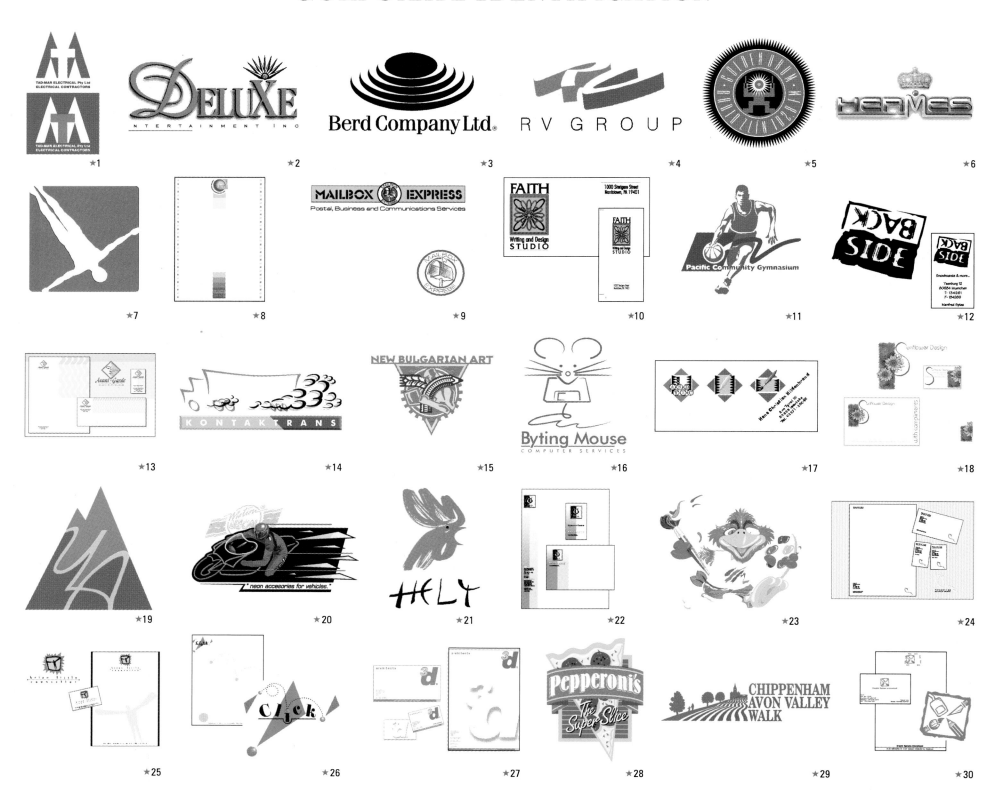

★1
★2
★3
★4
★5
★6
★7
★8
★9
★10
★11
★12
★13
★14
★15
★16
★17
★18
★19
★20
★21
★22
★23
★24
★25
★26
★27
★28
★29
★30

CORPORATE IDENTIFICATION

★1

★2

★3

★4

★5

★6

★7

★8

★9

★10

★11

12

★1

★7

★8

★9

★10

13

14

15

16

17

18

19

20

21

22

23

24

25

26

27

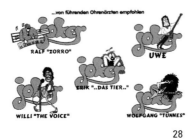
28

29

30

CORPORATE IDENTIFICATION

1

2

3

4

5

6

7

8

9

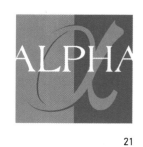

10

11

12

13

14

15

16

17

18

19

20

21

22

23

24

25

26

27

28

29

30

CORPORATE IDENTIFICATION

1

2

3

4

5

6

7

8

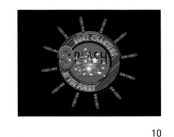

9

10

11

12

13

14

15

16

17

18

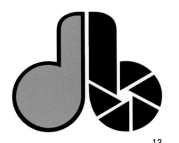

19

20

21

22

23

24

25

26

27

28

29

30

CORPORATE IDENTIFICATION

1

2

3

4

5

6

7

8

9

10

11

12

13

14

15

16

17

18

19

20

21

22

23

24

25

26

27

28

29

30

CORPORATE IDENTIFICATION

1

2

3

4

5

6

7

8

9

10

11

12

13

14

15

16

17

18

19

20

21

22

23

24

25

26

27

28

29

30

1

2

3

4

5

6

7

8

9

10

11

12

13

14

15

16

17

18

19

20

21

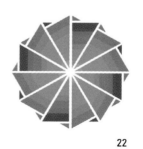

22

23

24

25

26

27

28

29

30

CORPORATE IDENTIFICATION

1

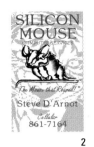

2

3

4

5

6

7

8

9

10

11

12

13

14

15

16

17

18

19

20

21

22

23

24

25

26

27

28

29

30

CORPORATE IDENTIFICATION

1

2

3

4

5

6

7

8

9

10

11

12

13

14

15

16

17

18

19

20

21

22

23

24

25

26

27

28

29

30

1

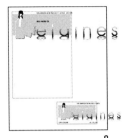

2

3

4

5

6

7

8

9

10

11

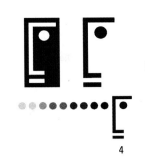

12

13

14

15

16

17

18

19

20

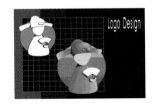

21

22

23

24

25

26

27

28

29

30

CORPORATE IDENTIFICATION

1

2

3

4

5

6

DEICMAR

7

8

9

10

FLÈCHE

11

12

MARK UP
Incentive Marketing

13

14

15

16

17

18

SWEET HOUSE

19

Vendramini

20

21

22

23

24

25

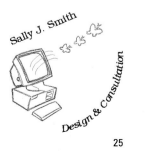

26

27

28

29

30

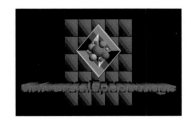

1

2

3

4

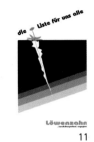

5

6

7

8

9

10

11

12

13

14

15

16

17

18

19

20

21

22

23

24

25

26

27

28

29

30

CORPORATE IDENTIFICATION

1

2

3

4

5

6

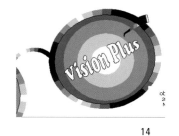

7

8

9

10

11

12

13

14

15

16

17

18

19

Yorkdale
Community Church

20

STILFLEX

STILFLEX

21

22

Manitoba
Computer Sciences Association Inc.

23

24

25

Fiesta

26

GUITAR FEST '94

GUITAR FEST '94

27

CHAMELEON
LIGHT
POWER & COLOR

28

JOKER
DISTRIBUTION

JOKER
DISTRIBUTION

JOKER
DISTRIBUTION

29

YSA
YOUNG SLOVAK ARTISTS

30

CORPORATE IDENTIFICATION

1

2

3

4

5

6

7

8

9

10

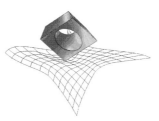

11

12

13

14

15

16

17

18

19

20

21

22

23

24

25

26

27

28

29

30

CORPORATE IDENTIFICATION

1

2

3

4

5

6

7

8

9

10

11

12

13

14

15

16

17

18

19

20

21

22

23

24

25

26

27

28

29

30

CORPORATE IDENTIFICATION

 PHOENIX COFFEE HOUSE
1

 OLIVE PATCH Authentic Italian Cuisine
2

 DÉPANNEUR Voisin
3

 PRODUCTIONS ÉTOILE
4

 DEM TEX INFORMATIQUE
5

 RISTORANTE TEVERE
6

 CAFÉ BILLARD CLUB PRIVÉ
7

 GeomaX
8

 Pirate Cola
9

 SPECGRAFIX DISTRIBUTION INC.
10

11

12

13

 Fawn Goulet, B.Sc., M.Sc. Research Associate — Goulet Medical Research Associates
14

 JOE'S COFFEE CO.
15

 Lincolnwood Training Club for German Shepherd Dogs, Inc. — All Breed Training • Obedience • Agility • Tracking
16

 HT HIGH TECH
17

 HT HIGH TECH
18

 TECHNOART computerized art & design
19

 BARLOW & ASSOCIATES CHARTERED QUANTITY SURVEYORS CONSTRUCTION COST CONSULTANTS PROJECT MANAGERS
20

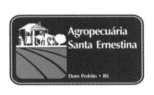 MASTER ASSURANCE
21

 Agropecuária Santa Ernestina Dom Pedrito • RS
22

 CELLULAR PHONE TELEFONIA MÓVEL CELULAR
23

 PANETTO PANS & DOCES
24

 VM viewer's marketplace
25

 HA! HA! HA! HA! HA! CARTOON Salomão
26

 FAIRVIEW PLACE HOME & Garden TOUR
27

 Jeannelle's Design
28

 Maprinca Materia Prima para la Industria c.a.
29

30

151

CORPORATE IDENTIFICATION

1

2

3

4

5

6

AD ArquiteturaDesign

7

8

9

10

11

12

the ALKING house

4211 US 1 South, Suite 140, St. Augustine, FL 32086   (904) 797-2897 - Ext. 101

13

14

15

16

17

18

19

20

21

22

23

24

25

26

27

28

29

30

CORPORATE IDENTIFICATION

1

2

3

4

5

6

7

8

9

10

11

12

13

14

15

16

17

18

19

20

21

22

23

24

25

26

27

28

29

30

CORPORATE IDENTIFICATION

1

2

3

4

5

6

7

8

9

10

11

12

13

14

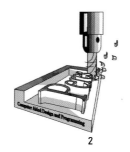

15

16

17

18

19

20

21

22

23

24

25

26

27

28

29

30

CORPORATE IDENTIFICATION

1

2

3

4

5

6

7

8

9

10

11

12

13

14

15

16

17

18

19

20

21

22

23

24

25

26

27

28

29

30

CORPORATE IDENTIFICATION

J.Scott Hamlin Design

1

HUDSON VALLEY COMMUNITY COLLEGE

2

PLANET OUR

3

Dallas Alley

4

CONFECCIONES

CONTINENTALES

5

HERRAMIENTAS Y CONSULTORIA AVANZADA S.A. DE C.V.

6

CATHABEL

7

new ENGLAND S.C.

NEW ENGLISH FOR EXECUTIVES

8

SNYDER PLASTICS INC.

9

21ST CENTURY DESIGN

10

21ST CENTURY DESIGN

11

MAKLA

Verkauf von Waren aller Art, insbesondere Textilien

12

Pontardawe Festival 1995 — The Story In The Song

13

Electromech Design, Inc.

EDI

903 N. Bowser, Suite 206 Richardson, TX 75081
Phone 214-644-0967 Fax 214-644-0980

14

BURLINGTON

INTERNATIONAL GAMES

15

BARLOW & ASSOCIATES

CHARTERED QUANTITY SURVEYORS
CONSTRUCTION COST CONSULTANTS
PROJECT MANAGERS

16

HAPPY DEVIL

17

SWEET HOUSE

18

TRAINING
IT
SERVICES

19

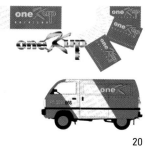

one cup

20

....country
WALLS

21

Giornalegiovani

22

TRATTO

GRAPHIC & DESIGN SERVICE

23

ИНСТАЛАЦИИ ОТОПЛИТЕЛНИ

24

25

FLY AFRICA
IN A 6 SEATER BEECH BARON
ADVENTURE SAFARIS FOR THE BUDGET TRAVELLER
MIKE HUDSON
NO 1 ST ANNES CRT CERES ROAD AVONDALE, HARARE ZIMBABWE
TEL: 963-4-339046

26

DSM

IT'S SURPRISING WHAT WE CAN DO TOGETHER

27

WINSKILL WATERMELONS

28

★1

★2

★3

★4

★5 OPTICAL SCIENCES CENTER THE UNIVERSITY OF ARIZONA

★6

★7

★8

★9

★10

★11 BADMINTON

★12

★13 THE LORD

★14 SPRING MUSKOKA

★15

★16 ADELAIDE HILLS BIG BAND

★17 Ferretti COMFORT

★18 GRUPPO FERRETTI

★19

★20

★21

★22 WATER POLO

★23

★24

★25

★26

★27 NOEL

★28

★29 Mikado

★30

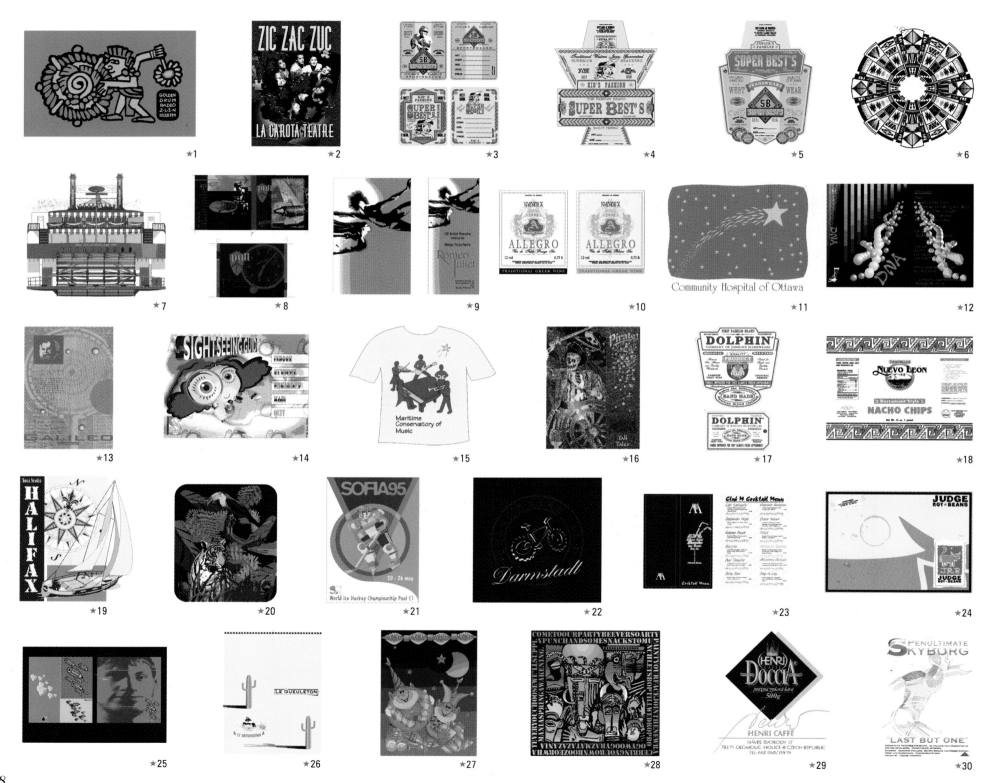

★1　★2　★3　★4　★5　★6

★7　★8　★9　★10　★11　★12

★13　★14　★15　★16　★17　★18

★19　★20　★21　★22　★23　★24

★25　★26　★27　★28　★29　★30

1

2

3

4

5

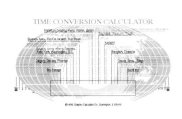

6

7

8

9

10

11

12

13

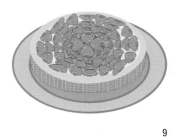

14

15

16

17

18

19

20

21

22

23

24

25

26

27

28

29

30

SPECIALTY AND LEISURE

1

2

3

4

5

6

7

8

9

10

11

12

13

14

15

16

17

18

19

20

21

22

23

24

25

26

27

28

29

30

1

2

3

4

5

6

7

8

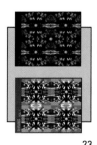

9

10

11

12

13

14

15

16

17

18

19

20

21

22

23

24

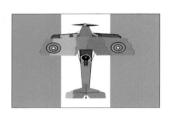

25

26

27

28

29

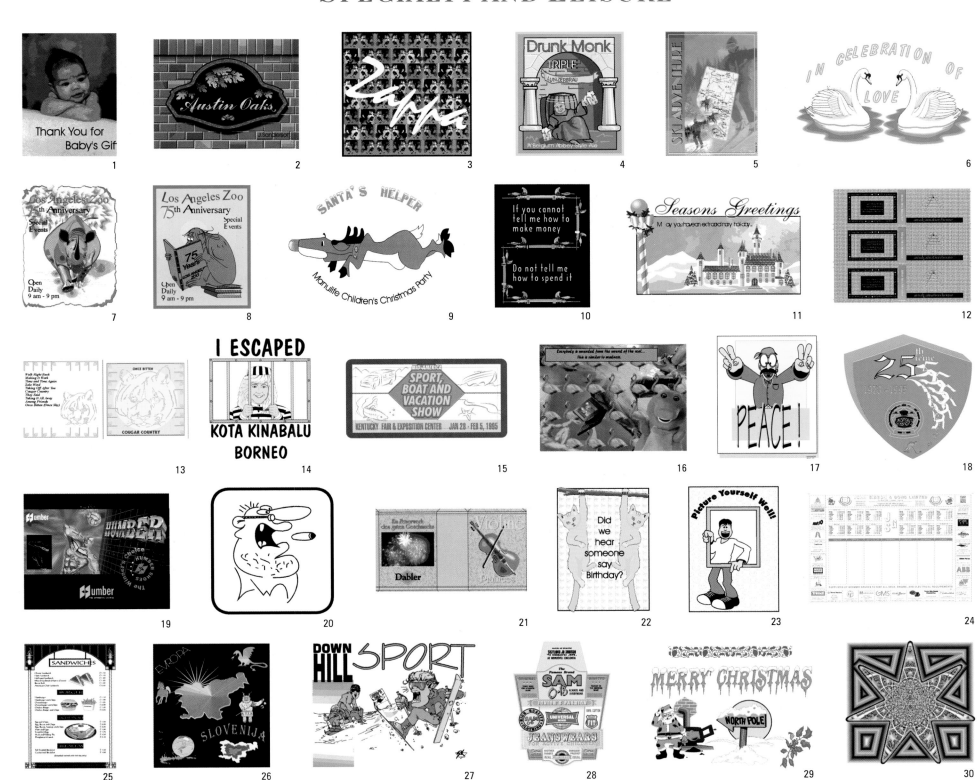

SPECIALTY AND LEISURE

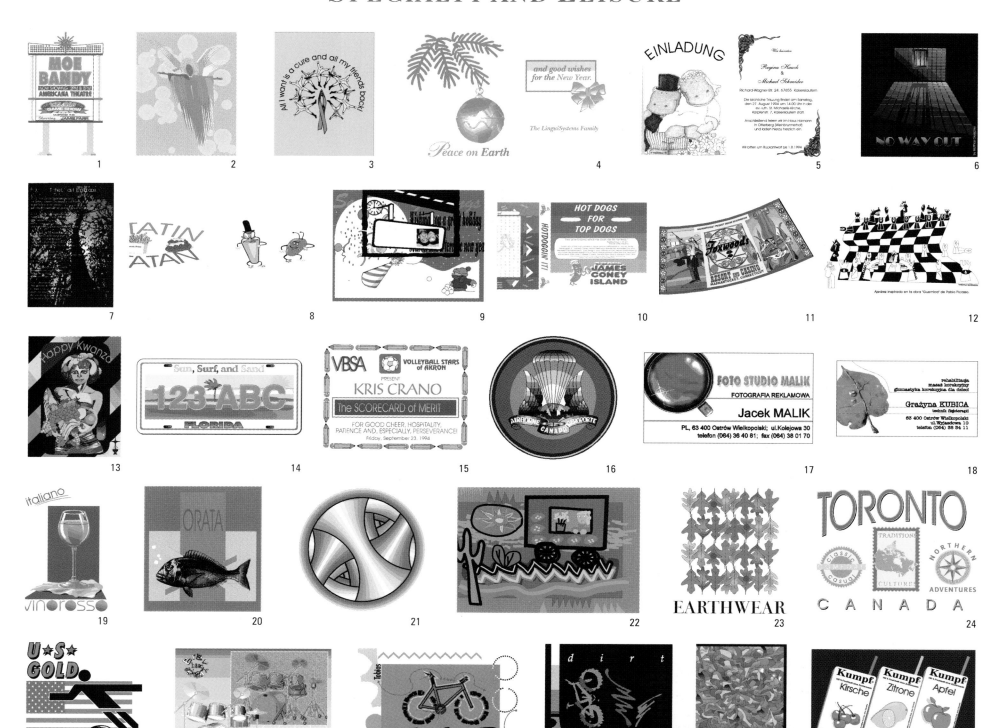

166

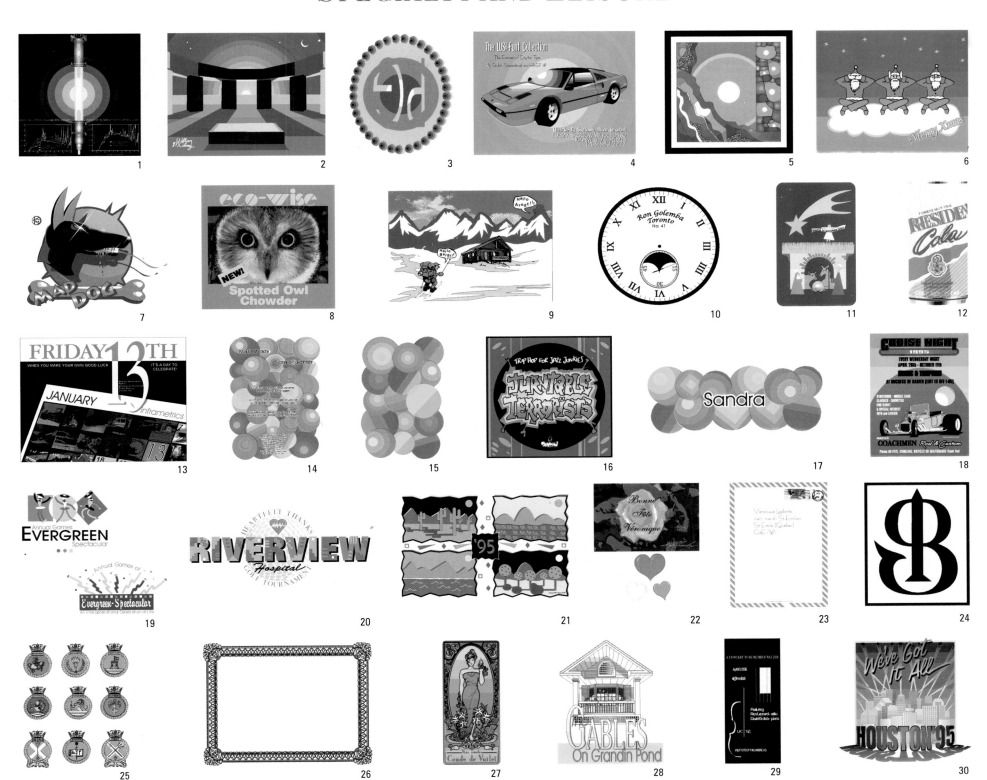

1

2

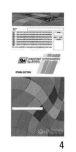

3

4

5

6

7

8

9

10

11

12

13

14

15

16

17

18

19

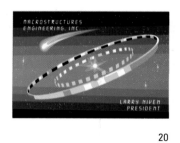

20

21

22

23

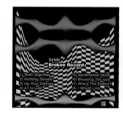

24

25

26

27

28

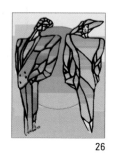

29

30

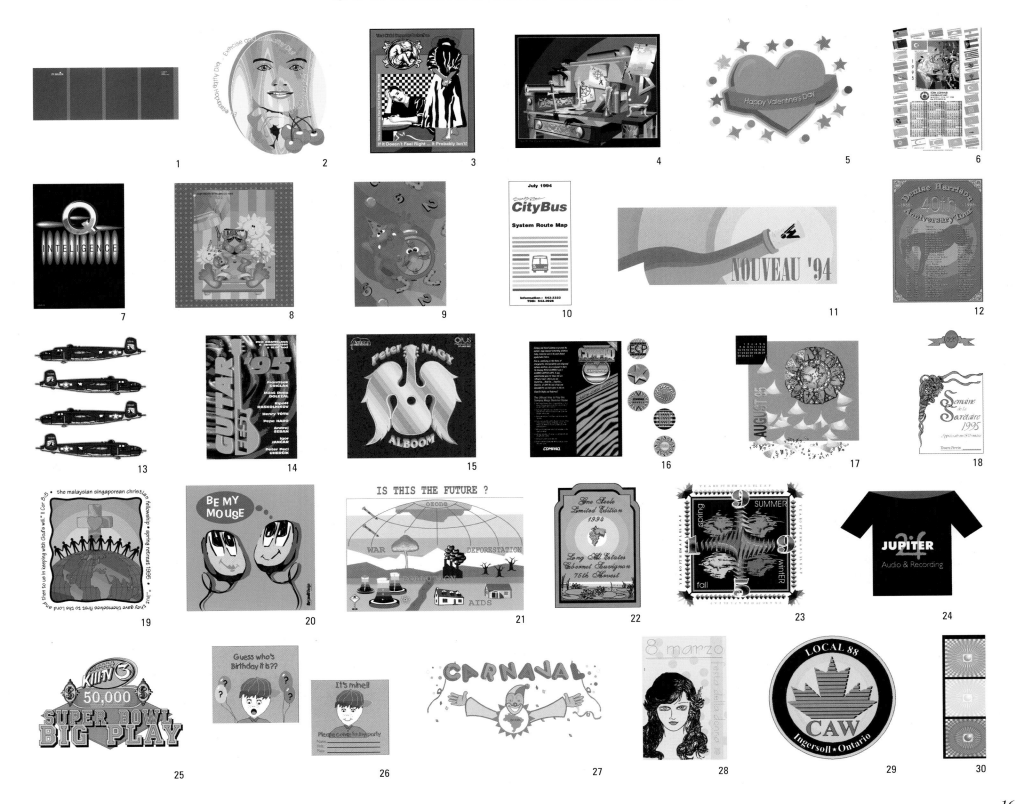

SPECIALTY AND LEISURE

1
2
3
4
5
6
7
8
9
10
11
12
13
14
15
16
17
18
19
20
21
22
23
24
25
26
27
28
29
30

SPECIALTY AND LEISURE

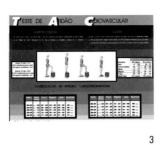

1

2

3

4

5

6

7

8

9

10

11

12

13

14

15

16

17

18

19

20

21

22

23

24

25

26

27

28

29

30

SPECIALTY AND LEISURE

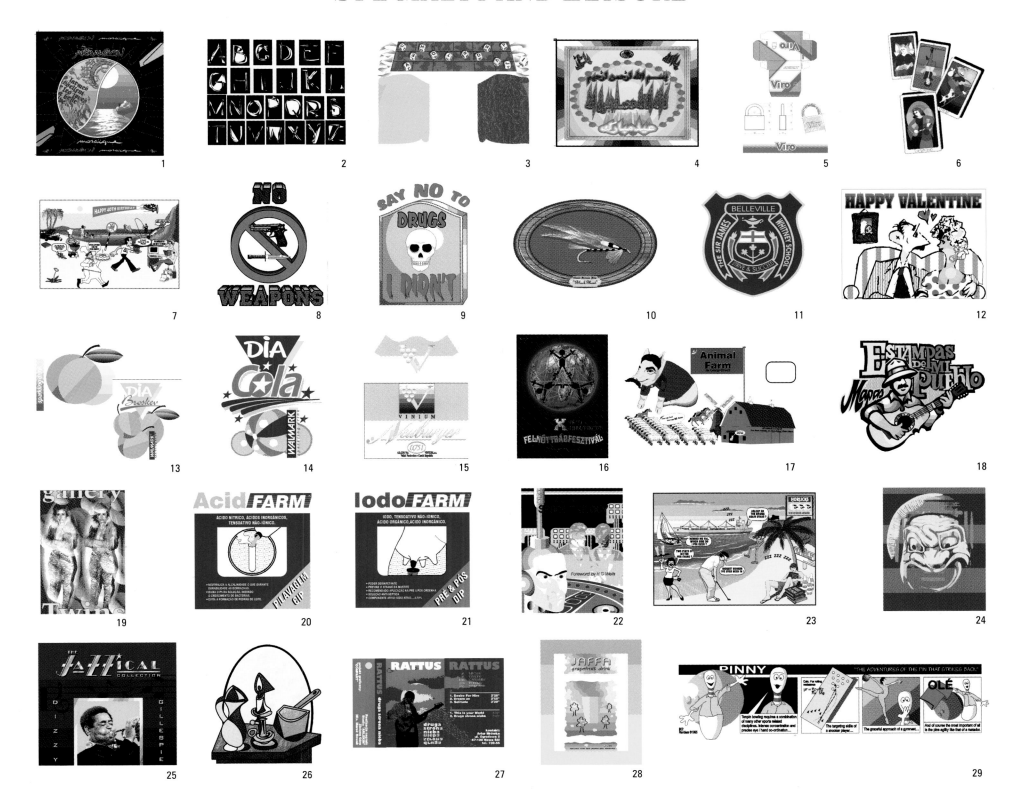

★1

★2

★3

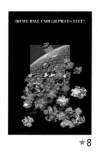

★4

★5

★6

★7

★8

★9

★10

★11

★12

★13

★14

★15

★16

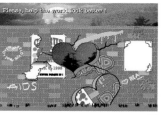

17

18

COREL PROFESSIONAL PHOTOS

★1 ★2 ★3 ★4 ★5 ★6

★7 8 9 10 11 12

13 14 15 16 17 18

19 20 21 22 23

24 25 26

175

$\mathcal{L}$IST OF ENTRIES

LIST OF ENTRIES

Welcome to Corel *ArtShow* 6.

The Corel *ArtShow* 6 CD-ROM showcases a selection of over 2,600 high-quality designs entered in the Sixth Annual Corel World Design Contest.

If you do not have CorelDRAW installed on your system, the Corel *ArtShow* 6 CD-ROM provides flexible image management applications for Windows 3.1x, Windows 95 and Macintosh platforms. These applications allow you to view the images, organize them into albums, view them in slide shows and much more.

Normally requiring over 2.6 gigabytes of storage space, these designs have been placed on a single CD-ROM using special compression techniques.

If you already have CorelDRAW 5 or CorelDRAW 6 installed, a modified import filter will be installed into your existing copy of CorelDRAW. This new filter will allow you to unlock the wonders of *ArtShow* 6.

To view the images please follow the instruction as explained in the Corel *ArtShow* 6 CD-ROM booklet.

Grand Prize World

Designer	File Name	City	Country	Telephone Number
Page 1				
Radim Mojzis	CHA00729	Vsetin	Czech Republic	42-657-81499
Page 3				
Robert Travers	PE000504	Montreal	Canada	514-482-2280
Page 5				
John M. Morris	LAN01313	Sound Beach	U.S.A.	516 744 86 93
Page 7				
Michael Koester	PRO00615	Goeppingen	Germany	49-7-161-428-47
Page 9				
Theodor Ushev	PAG00984	Sofia	Bulgaria	359-2-65-88-51
Page 11				
Radim Mojzis	COR00189	Vsetin	Czech Republic	42-657-81499
Page 13				
Amedeo Gigli	SPE00938	Rome	Italy	39-6-8810-710
Page 15				
Matthias Gleirscher	PHO00600	Neustift	Austria	43-5226-2600
Page 17				
Valorie Lennox	MOV00523	Salt Springs	Canada	604-537-5145
Page 19				
Jim Bisakowski/Lee Gabel	VEN00520	Victoria	Canada	604-383-8622
Page 21				
Silvio Martins Alegre	PRO01093	Rio de Janeiro	Brazil	55-21-246-8671
Page 23				
Alexandre Kojouchner	LAN01208	Odessa	Ukraine	380-64-97-20

Monthly Contest Winners

Designer	File Name	City	Country	Telephone Number
Page 24				
Jerry Brown	PE000886	Farmington Hills	U.S.A.	810-442-7373
Page 25				
Robert Travers	PE001458	Montreal	Canada	514-482-2280
Page 26				
Huan Le Tran	PE000506	Toronto	Canada	416-462-0906
Page 27				
Andreas Sewald	PE000673	Jork	Germany	49-41-62-6705
Page 28				
Ceri Lines	PE000929	Hsinchu	Taiwan	886-35-772-155
Page 29				
Georgina Curry/Gerry Moss	PE001319	Scottsdale	U.S.A.	602-443-8786
Page 30				
Huan Le Tran	PE000850	Toronto	Canada	416-462-0906
Page 31				
Gerry Wilson	LAN00015	Brooklyn	U.S.A.	718-836-9181
Page 32				
Gustavo A. Ortiz Serrano	LAN00126	Satafe de Bogata	Columbia	011 571-210-4259
Page 33				
Antonio De Leo	LAN01005	Rome	Italy	39-6-9700-322
Page 34				
Jerry Brown	LAN000562	Farmington Hills	U.S.A.	810-442-7373
Page 35				
Fabio Gargitter	LAN01393	Sao Paulo	Brazil	55-11-288-3341
Page 36				
Tomasz Wawrzyczek	LAN00803	Rybnik	Poland	48-36-28557
Page 37				
Matthew Lecher	LAN01051	Newcastle	U.S.A.	207-865-4171
Page 38				
Francesco Vavassori	PRO00091	Bonate Sotto	Italy	39-35-99-3555
Page 39				
John M. Morris	PRO00113	Sound Beach	U.S.A.	516-744-8693
Page 40				
Klaus Hennig	PRO00278	Leonberg	Germany	49-71-522-60-7172
Page 41				
Cedric Bonhommeau	PRO00726	Cornille	France	33-1-99-49-60-38
Page 42				
Michael Bruggeman	PRO00777	St. Henry	U.S.A.	513-255-6739
Page 43				
Stefano Maugeri	PRO01086	Modena	Italy	39-59-37-05-95
Page 44				
Enrico Tomaselli	PRO01298	Rome	Italy	39-6-214-7909
Page 45				
Gabriele Homolka	PAG00097	Stuttgart	Germany	49-711-649-2215
Page 46				
Marion Frank/Klaus Hennig	PAG00163	Leonberg	Germany	49-7152-260-7172
Page 47				
Jean Lawler	PAG00320-321	North Bend	U.S.A.	206-888-1667
Page 48				
Mary Endress	PAG00629	Toronto	Canada	416-960-2764
Page 49				
Rick Mank	PAG00885	Toronto	Canada	416-960-7115
Page 50				
Montserrat Noguera Montades	PAG01280	Barcelona	Spain	34-3-487-12-80
Page 51				
Miriam Randall Morrison	PAG01616-1618	Putnam	U.S.A.	860-928-6042
Page 52				
Josef Valek/Milan Matous	COR00097	Valasske	Czech Republic	42-651 -2171 6
Page 53				
Radim Mojzis	COR00189	Vsetin	Czech Republic	011 42-657-81499
Page 54				
Piotr Lopatka	COR00316	Ostrow	Poland	48-64-36-75-71
Page 55				
Edward Cristina	COR00608	Ottawa	Canada	613-237-0158
Page 56				
René Ebert	COR00732	Kamenz	Germany	49-3578-5821
Page 57				
Mike Sturba/Russell Wilson	COR00968	Windsor	Canada	519-971-0445
Page 58				
Peter & John Reddy	COR01178	Dublin	Ireland	353-1-496-2000
Page 59				
Romain Maffei	SPE00088	Lausanne	Switzerland	41-21-653-8200
Page 60				
Radim Mojzis	SPE00211	Vsetin	Czech Republic	011 42-657-81499
Page 61				
Chris Purcell	SPE00531	Houston	U.S.A.	713-374-4679
Page 62				
Eric Smith	SPE00627	Brampton	Canada	905-792-1981
Page 63				
Chris Purcell	SPE01052	Houston	U.S.A.	713-374-4679
Page 64				
Rick Mank (Designer)	SPE01240-1243	Toronto	Canada	416-960-2764
Page 65				
Filho Salomao	SPE01909	Sao Paulo	Brazil	55-11-881-2448

Best of the Americas

Designer	File Name	City	Country	Telephone Number
Page 66				
1. Wil Dawson	PE000807	Tulsa	U.S.A.	918-234-1362
2. Huan Le Tran	PE001410	Toronto	Canada	416-462-0906
3. Tibirica Altamiro Dias	PE000801	Belo Horizonte	Brazil	52-3-620-3926
Page 67				
1. James-Michael G. Harlan	SPE01834	Brighton	U.S.A.	810-486-3964
2. Jerry Brown	COR01772	Farmington Hills	U.S.A.	810-442-7373
3. Alejandro Urzua Espinosa	PE001132	Guadalajara	Mexico	55-31-443-5829

Best of Europe and the Rest of the World

Designer	File Name	City	Country	Telephone Number
Page 68				
1. Radim Mojzis	COR01678	Vsetin	Czech Republic	011 42-657-81499
2. Lie Tjeng Kian	PE001256	Bandung	Indonesia	62-22-303-286
3. Amedeo Gigli	PE001395	Rome	Italy	39-6-8810-710
Page 69				
1. Alain Marchand	PE000817	Le Havre	France	33-35-21-15-10
2. Horst Haas	PE000881	Gummersbach	Germany	49-2261-52454
3. Dalia Levin	PE000678	Rehovot	Israel	972-8-466-795
Page 70				
Robert Boutin	INH00009	Ottawa	Canada	613-728-0826
Page 71				
Georgina Curry	INDIAN	Scottsdale	U.S.A.	602-443-8786
Page 72				
Bill Frymire	REX	Vancouver	Canada	604-875-9880
Page 73				
Steve Lyons	HORSEMAN	Fairfax	U.S.A.	415-555-1212
Page 74				
David Brickley	DIVERS	Portland	U.S.A.	503-236-4883

People, Plants and Animals

Designer	File Name	City	Country	Telephone Number
Page 76				
1.Francesc Verdu	Peo00007	Mutxamel	Spain	96-565-9917
2.Gustavo A. Ortiz Serrano	Peo00009	Santafe de Bogota	Colombia	57-1-2104243
3.Janusz Szewczyk	Peo00014	Lodz	Poland	57-25-84
4.Francesco Vavassori	Peo00018	Bonate Sotto	Italy	035-99-3555
5.Michael Degen	Peo00027	Heinsberg	Germany	49-2452-21110
6.Pierre Kleinholtz	Peo00031	St. Ciers d'Abzac	France	57-69-00-64
7.Jefferson Martins de Barros	Peo00045	Rio de Janeiro	Brazil	55021-225-8305
8.Hans Peter Kauth	Peo00048	Hamburg	Germany	040-850-86-35
9.Lee Joseph G. Favis	Peo00077	Scarborough	Canada	416-286-6250
10.Hannes Stepper	Peo00082	Berg	Germany	09189-7381
11.Piotr Lopatka	Peo00084	Ostrow Wielkopolski	Poland	064-36-75-71
12.Guenther Grauel	Peo00093	Gudensberg	Germany	05603-3683
13.Anthony King	Peo00098	Teddington	United Kingdom	181-943-1526
14.Giacomo Pirro	Peo00099	Martinengo	Italy	363-988-830
15.Gerry Wilson	Peo00107	Brooklyn	U.S.A.	718-836-9181
16.Richard Donato	Peo00122	Chicago	U.S.A.	312-427-4520
17.Rob Bird	Peo00143	Kenilworth	United Kingdom	01926 58042
18.Harri Pulli	Peo00147	Oulu	Finland	358- 81-510241
19.Stephen Arscott	Peo00148	Mississauga	Canada	905-896-4664
20.Adim Martin Ebube	Peo00149	Hyattsville	U.S.A.	301-699-8528
21.Xavier Bisbe i Serra	Peo00169	Torroella De Montgi	Spain	72-75 72 54
22.Rhonda S. Keene	Peo00170	Poughquag	U.S.A.	914-724-5156
23.Ryszard Bukanski	Peo00173	Gorzow WLKP	Poland	095-324-176
24.Gerry Wilson	Peo00182	Brooklyn	U.S.A.	718-836-9181
25.Gerry Wilson	Peo00183	Brooklyn	U.S.A.	718-836-9181
26.Michael Jukes	Peo00190	Reno	U.S.A.	702-829-0935
27.Simon Jelks	Peo00199	Dundee	Scotland	0382 825629
28.	Peo00211			
29.Johan Widegren	Peo00502	Vasteras	Sweden	46-21-189-374
30.Francesco Verdu	Peo00505	Mutxamel	Spain	96-565-9917
Page 77				
1.Remi Forcier	Peo00525	Vancouver	Canada	604-685-7696
2.Jay/Rhonda Keene	Peo00538	Poughquag	U.S.A.	914-724-5156
3.Cedric Bonhommeau	Peo00560	Cornille	France	99-49-6038
4.Robert Rusick	Peo00568	Rochester	U.S.A.	716-461-5038
5.Michael Breunig	Peo00569	Leverkusen	Germany	n/a
6.Scott D. Crane	Peo00602	Alexandria	U.S.A.	703-922-0860
7.Rene Arlt	Peo00616	Berlin	Germany	030-721-3023
8.Helge/Sven Ulrich	Peo00618	Poughquag	U.S.A.	914-724-5156
9.Jay/Rhonda Keene	Peo00628	Kamenz	Germany	03578-5821
10.Fabrice Geelen	Peo00656	Liege	Belgium	041-442-668
11.Remi Forcier	Peo00665	Vancouver	Canada	604-685-7696
12.Dan Brown	Peo00683	Vancouver	Canada	206-737-9920
13.Stephen Arscott	Peo00686	Mississauga	Canada	905-896-4664
14.Eric Moss	Peo00710	Harrogate	England	423-525-807
15.Michael Neary	Peo00721	Neuilly-sur-Seine	France	33-1-4747-7177
16.Jose Luis P. Fiweiredo	Peo00741	Rio de Janeiro	Brazil	021-270-8286
17.Gustavo A. Ortiz Serrano	Peo00765	Santafe de Bogota	Colombia	57-1-2104243
18.Addam Ooi	Peo00776	Kuala Lumpur	Malaysia	03-9311930
19.Lavinia Martini	Peo00789	Rome	Italy	39-6-8121-653
20.Marcia Henderson	Peo00815	Elm Grove	U.S.A.	318-742-7645
21.Dave Wingard	Peo00818	Portland	U.S.A.	503-257-6574
22.Georges Pelletier	Peo00821	Brossard	Canada	514-656-3919
23.Georges Pelletier	Peo00822	Brossard	Canada	514-656-3919
24.Georges Pelletier	Peo00823	Brossard	Canada	514-656-3919
25.Georges Pelletier	Peo00824	Brossard	Canada	514-656-3919
26.Georges Pelletier	Peo00825	Brossard	Canada	514-656-3919
27.Marin/Neil Darmonkow	Peo00831	St. John's	Canada	709-747-0140
28.Norbert Pachler	Peo00843	Maeder	Austria	n/a
29.Alice Mininch	Peo00851	Nepean	Canada	613-727-5696
30.Philip Yeung Sin Lee	Peo00867	Kwai Chung	Hong Kong	852-24 24 34 25
Page 78				
1.Donna Wandel	Peo00868	Derby	U.S.A.	203-734-1369
2.	Peo00876			n/a
3.Teresa Pistora	Peo00928	Salina	U.S.A.	913-825-8769
4.Jorn Paessler	Peo00938	Erlangen	Germany	011-49-9131-602-987
5.Addam Ooi	Peo00969	Kuala Lumpur	Malaysia	03-9311930
6.Philip Townsley	Peo00972	Bournemouth	United Kingdom	44 1202 532 959
7.Markus Koote	Peo01030	Oberhausen	Germany	0208-677993
8.Cecil G. Rice	Peo01060	Acworth	U.S.A.	404-974-0684
9.Francis Rubin	Peo01074	Lima	Peru	5114-447-4326
10.Montserrat Noguera Muntadas	Peo01103	Barcelona	Spain	487-1280
11.Samuel Czukerberg	Peo01109	Mexico	Mexico	525-540-7465
12.Jody Robertson-Schramm	Peo01113	Chelmsford	U.S.A.	508-250-0374
13.Josef Prchal	Peo01126	Heideck	Germany	09177-9551
14.Jefferson Martins de Barros	Peo01241	Rio de Janeiro	Brazil	55021-225-8305
15.Hans-Joachim Kardinal	Peo01296	Berlin	Germany	030-431-0306
16.Elana Tontini	Peo01320	Anzio	Italy	39-6-9865444
17.Georgina Curry	Peo01371	Scottsdale	U.S.A.	602-443-8786
18.Jerry Brown	Peo01407	Farmington Hills	U.S.A.	810-442-7373
19.Elizabeth Jassem	Peo01413	Mississauga	Canada	905-566-0158
20.Andrew Welson	Peo01429	Edmonton	Canada	403-484-5468
21.Rainer Muellner	Peo01438	Berghuelen 2	Germany	
22.Gilberto Guajardo	Peo01439	Monterrey	U.S.A.	528-346-8991
23.Teri Paulus	Peo01441	Grass Valley	U.S.A.	916-273-4682
24.Kitisak Ratanalerthada	Peo01443	Bangkok	Thailand	066-2-377-6316
25.Pawel Bodytk	Peo01445	Colleyville	U.S.A.	817 421-1150
26.Tamas Hajas	Peo01446	Szeged	Hungary	36 62-434-519
27.Tamas Hajas	Peo01447	Szeged	Hungary	36 62-434-519
28.Greg Maunder	Peo01448	Port Perry	Canada	905-985-9961
29.Marijke de Wendt	Peo01454	Haarlem	Netherlands	023-313424
30.Marijke de Wendt	Peo01455	Haarlem	Netherlands	023-313424

LIST OF ENTRIES

People, Plants and Animals

Page 79

Designer	File Name	City	Country	Telephone Number
1.Bruce W. Jones	Peo00075	Atlanta	U.S.A.	404-875-1517
2.Dieudonne Heeren	Peo00079	Hoogerheide	Netherlands	31-01646-1588
3.Edward Volchok	Peo00080	Brooklyn	U.S.A.	718-252-5445
4.Hannes Stepper	Peo00082	Berg	Germany	09189-7381
5.Steven Van Der Merwe	Peo00083	Glenwood	South Africa	031-216956
6.Jurgen Schumacher	Peo00085	Berlin	Germany	030-9320277
7.Jolanta Romanowska	Peo00087	Warsaw	Poland	24-38-69
8.Franz Aschwanden	Peo00088	Bremgarten	Switzerland	57-37-76-26
9.Alex Blomsma	Peo00089	Schoonrewoerd	Netherlands	31-3454-2115
10.Mike Cucksey	Peo00090	Birkenhead	United Kingdom	51 647 2366
11.Mike Cucksey	Peo00091	Birkenhead	United Kingdom	51 647 2366
12.Guenther Grauel	Peo00094	Gudensberg	Germany	05603-3683
13.Juergen Bradt	Peo00095	Hildesheim	Germany	05121-12821
14.George Scott Smalley	Peo00097	Frankfort	U.S.A.	502-875-4460
15.Terry Blackburn	Peo00100	Hillsboro	U.S.A.	503-640-3371
16.Bradley Bannister	Peo00101	Huntsville	U.S.A.	205-539-0186
17.Patrick Lichty	Peo00105	N. Canton	U.S.A.	216-494-5593
18.Salah Benferroudtj	Peo00108	Montreuil	France	48-55-62-97
19.Salah Benferroudtj	Peo00109	Montreuil	France	48-55-62-97
20.Salah Benferroudtj	Peo00110	Montreuil	France	48-55-62-97
21.Marco Machinek	Peo00111	Bremen	Germany	04921-4675907
22.Guido Blank	Peo00113	Rio Do Sul	Brazil	0478-21-0203
23.Emmanuel D'Esparbes	Peo00115	Saint Gilles	France	262-240710
24.Karl-Heinz Pfefferer	Peo00118	Wemding	Germany	n/a
25.Pedro de Souza Silva	Peo00120	Rio de Janeiro	Brazil	55-21-252-8167
26.W. Bruce Funderburk	Peo00123	Charlotte	U.S.A.	704-333-9011
27.Matt McCarthy	Peo00124	Scottsdale	U.S.A.	602-998-9437
28.Elsa Cals Brugger	Peo00125	Rio de Janeiro	Brazil	5521-325-2888
29.Holzknecht Heinz	Peo00126	Seefeld	Austria	052-1-24300
30.Bruce W. Jones	Peo00137	Atlanta	U.S.A.	404-875-1517

Page 80

Designer	File Name	City	Country	Telephone Number
1.Enrico Tomaselli	Peo00138	Rome	Italy	214-7909
2.Roger Bruienne	Peo00139	Rheinberg	Germany	n/a
3.Michel Dupuis	Peo00145	St-Basile	Canada	514-653-6691
4.Christian-Michael Mark	Peo00150	Herne	Germany	02325-62719
5.Wolf D. Rosenblatt	Peo00152	Mittelbrunn	Germany	06371-16973
6.Wolf D. Rosenblatt	Peo00159	Mittelbrunn	Germany	06371-16973
7.Arthur Hollmann	Peo00161	Glattbach	Germany	n/a
8.Petra Jungblut	Peo00163	Berlin	Germany	030-813-1942
9.Wolfgang H. Sator	Peo00167	Essen	Germany	0201-500-349
10.Hans Jorgen Wevers	Peo00168	Monchengladbach	Germany	021-61-209-112
11.Ryszard Bukanski	Peo00177	Gorzow WLKP	Poland	095-324-176
12.Michael J. Barnes	Peo00179	Canon City	U.S.A.	719-275-2102
13.Wil Dawson	Peo00180	Tulsa	U.S.A.	918-234-1362
14.Bill Tillman	Peo00181	Sandy	U.S.A.	503-668-8505
15.Ken Schwartz	Peo00184	Omaha	U.S.A.	402-558-5517
16.Wongtawan Chaiyakul	Peo00185	Virginia Beach	U.S.A.	804-496-9503
17.Frank Roth	Peo00188	Hunstetten 2	Germany	06126-8989
18.Matt Mawson	Peo00191	Ashgrove	Australia	617-366-2069
19.Vagelis Michelidacis	Peo00192	Athens	Greece	1905-465-6749
20.Rose Marie Krebsbach	Peo00194	Mequon	U.S.A.	414-242-2200
21.Carlo Doneda	Peo00195	Bergamo	Italy	035-313-333
22.Jason J. Coor	Peo00201	Lincoln	U.S.A.	402-477-9408
23.Frits W. Godin	Peo00203	Harbor City	U.S.A.	310-830-0175
24.Wil Dawson	Peo00212	Tulsa	U.S.A.	918-234-1362
25.Mogens Buro	Peo00213	Stenungsund	Sweden	46 303 83328
26.John Lait	Peo00517	Vancouver	Canada	604-669-9570
27.Gunter Weber	Peo00521	GroBrosseln	Germany	n/a
28.Joe C. Werner	Peo00524	Pleasant Hill	U.S.A.	510-228-3522
29.Martin Machnowski	Peo00526	Big Rapids	U.S.A.	616-592-6435
30.Adim Martin Ebube	Peo00527	Hyattsville	U.S.A.	301-699-8528

Page 81

Designer	File Name	City	Country	Telephone Number
1.Richard Dewar	Peo00528	Aberdeen	Scotland	01044-224-771444
2.Pedro de Souza Silva	Peo00529	Rio de Janeiro	Brazil	55-21-252-8167
3.Douglas Schoeffler	Peo00530	Redmond	U.S.A.	206-556-9511
4.Douglas Schoeffler	Peo00531	Redmond	U.S.A.	206-556-9511
5.Douglas Schoeffler	Peo00532	Redmond	U.S.A.	206-556-9511
6.Sergio de Sena Tavares	Peo00535	Rio de Janeiro	Brazil	021-591-1842
7.Luz Earley	Peo00537	Irving	U.S.A.	214-438-3907
8.Palle Pederson	Peo00539	Karslunde	Denmark	45-421-51619
9.Olaga Heffner	Peo00540	Bellwood	U.S.A.	708-547-9491
10.William J. Sutherland	Peo00541	Regina	Canada	306-352-6757
11.Laurie McCanna	Peo00543	Pacifica	U.S.A.	415-359-7794
12.Andre Perreault	Peo00544	New Westminster	Canada	604-528-6261
13.Richardo Cateriano Zapater	Peo00546	Lima	Peru	0051-14-222702
14.Ilona Reiners	Peo00574	Bruhl	Germany	02232-22668
15.Bayu Santiko	Peo00549	Tegal	Indonesia	n/a
16.Bayu Santiko	Peo00550	Tegal	Indonesia	n/a
17.Larry L. Pool	Peo00551	Des Moines	U.S.A.	515-285-5378
18.Kevin Landis	Peo00556	Reseda	U.S.A.	818-609-9320
19.Willem Zwaard	Peo00557	Abcoude	Netherlands	02946-3204
20.Kuapil Ales	Peo00558	C. Budejovice	Czech Republic	n/a
21.Sijham Bahri	Peo00559	Silver Spring	U.S.A.	301-680-8912
22.James MacGregor	Peo00561	Surrey	Canada	604-596-8154
23.Barry Long	Peo00562	Franklin	U.S.A.	615-794-0164
24.Dominique Bertrand	Peo00565	Longueil	Canada	514-646-5447
25.Richard Leonetti	Peo00567	Portland	U.S.A.	503-246-4952
26.Arthur Hollmann	Peo00570	Glattbach	Germany	n/a
27.Ilona Reiners	Peo00572	Bruhl	Germany	02232-22668
28.Ilona Reiners	Peo00573	Bruhl	Germany	02232-22668
29.Ilona Reiners	Peo00578	Bruhl	Germany	02232-22668
30.Willi Hagmeyer	Peo00579	Essen	Germany	0201-501-497

People, Plants and Animals

Page 82

Designer	File Name	City	Country	Telephone Number
1.Mathias Wien	Peo00581	Hitzhofen	Germany	08458-9929
2.Phi Hung Le	Peo00583	Lognes	France	60.17.78.31
3.Igor Hristov	Peo00590	Bourgas	Bulgaria	66 12 79
4.G. Philip Angel	Peo00591	Marietta	U.S.A.	404-565-6257
5.Frank Dietrich	Peo00593	Tallahassee	U.S.A.	904-671-1529
6.Wendy Starita-Mathews	Peo00594	Bridgeview	U.S.A.	708-598-7323
7.Robert Hammond	Peo00595	Bogart	U.S.A.	706-613-6974
8.Joselito Macapagal	Peo00596	Richmond	Canada	604-276-4578
9.Andreas Rose	Peo00597	Bremervorde	Germany	04764-1022
10.Rodolfo Francisco Ponce	Peo00598	Haedo	Argentina	659-3646
11.Rodolfo Francisco Ponce	Peo00599	Haedo	Argentina	659-3646
12.Rodolfo Francisco Ponce	Peo00601	Haedo	Argentina	659-3646
13.Reed Fisher	Peo00604	San Clemente	U.S.A.	714-498-0634
14.Jose Luis P. Finneiredo	Peo00607	Rio de Janeiro	Brazil	n/a
15.Eva Kleinhans	Peo00620	Kaufbeuren	Germany	08341-61414
16.	Peo00622			
17.Stanislawa Dobrzeniecka	Peo00623	Szczecin	Poland	4891-526043
18.Elsa Cals Brugger	Peo00629	Rio de Janeiro	Brazil	5521-325-2888
19.Rene Ebert	Peo00630	Kamenz	Germany	03578-5821
20.Rene Ebert	Peo00631	Kamenz	Germany	03578-5821
21.Rene Ebert	Peo00632	Kamenz	Germany	03578-5821
22.Jens Fechter	Peo00642	Windesheim	Germany	06707-1404
23.Christa Reisinger	Peo00643	Himmelried	Switzerland	n/a
24.Thomas Tintschl	Peo00645	Frankfurt	Germany	n/a
25.Thomas Enrich	Peo00648	Bosenbach	Germany	06385-1836
26.Ana Paula Salotti	Peo00649	Rio de Janeiro	Brazil	55-21-439-9109
27.Rafal Werszler	Peo00658	Wroclaw	Poland	071 481750
28.Rafal Werszler	Peo00659	Wroclaw	Poland	071 481750
29.Stephen James Liddiard	Peo00662	Barrie	Canada	705-739-6230
30.Sensini Aimerys	Peo00663	Cesena	Italy	0547-330493

Page 83

Designer	File Name	City	Country	Telephone Number
1.Bela Trussel-Cullen	Peo00664	Auckland	New Zealand	64-9-376-7190
2.Charlotte Faber	Peo00666	Amstelveen	Netherlands	(0)20-6418257
3.Americo Vigorita	Peo00667	Yonkers	U.S.A.	914-968-1683
4.Mark Norwood	Peo00669	Baltimore	U.S.A.	410-366-4926
5.Michael Sukes	Peo00670	Reno	U.S.A.	702-746-8505
6.Michael Grenz	Peo00674	Schwindegg	Germany	08082-8116
7.Peter Simmons	Peo00676	Norwich	United Kingdom	01603 616292
8.Ken Farrar	Peo00682	Kamloops	Canada	604-828-0440
9.Donna Peet	Peo00684	Dunedin	U.S.A.	813-736-6371
10.Victoria E. Riley	Peo00685	Cincinnati	U.S.A.	513-742-5691
11.Montserrat Noguera Muntadas	Peo00687	Barcelona	Spain	487-1280
12.Linky De Bruyn	Peo00688	Waterkloof Park	South Africa	27-12-469-646
13.Salah Benferroudj	Peo00690	Montreuil	France	68-55-62-92
14.Luiz Eduardo de Oliveira	Peo00692	Rio de Janeiro	Brazil	21-294-8756
15.Ken Dove	Peo00696	Calgary	Canada	403-274-6296
16.Jerry Wilson	Peo00699	Brooklyn	U.S.A.	718-836-9181
17.Alvaro Sanchez-Vicente	Peo00700	Bilbao	Spain	94-4457985
18.Richard Clothier	Peo00703	Windlesham	United Arab Emirates	01276-476-423
19.Simone Pampado	Peo00704	Frassinelle	Italy	39-425-933-117
20.Harri Hietala	Peo00705	Kemi	Finland	358-698-220-731
21.Michael Harris	Peo00707	Stoke-On-Trent	United Kingdom	01782 333 783
22.Stefano Blasi	Peo00713	Rome	Italy	39-6-3227369
23.Frits W. Godin	Peo00714	Harbour City	U.S.A.	310-830-0175
24.Robert Hammond	Peo00716	Bogart	U.S.A.	706-613-6974
25.Salvado Gunnar Kossatz	Peo00719	Hamburg	Germany	49 40 430 7788
26.Robert Rasmussen	Peo00724	Skanderborg	Denmark	86 510351
27.Albert America	Peo00725	Zurich	Switzerland	01-272-1848
28.Rodney Knoke	Peo00727	Green Bay	U.S.A.	414-499-5031
29.Chuck McCrory	Peo00728	Maple Shade	U.S.A.	609-779-9702
30.Robert Muller	Peo00729	Oldenburg	Germany	n/a

Page 84

Designer	File Name	City	Country	Telephone Number
1.Willem Zwaard	Peo00731	Abcoude	Netherlands	02946-3204
2.Barto Farrar	Peo00732	Fort Worth	U.S.A.	817-834-1162
3.Maria S. Campos	Peo00733	Fontana	U.S.A.	909-899-0088
4.Reinhard Groning	Peo00735	Willich	Germany	02154-42058
5.Ray Williams	Peo00743	Longview	U.S.A.	360-577-4374
6.Carlo Doneda	Peo00747	Bergamo	Italy	035 31 33 33
7.Luciano Boiteux, Milena Matto	Peo00748	Rio de Janeiro	Brazil	n/a
8.Luciano Boiteux, Milena Matto	Peo00749	Rio de Janeiro	Brazil	n/a
9.Luciano Boiteux, Milena Matto	Peo00750	Rio de Janeiro	Brazil	n/a
10.Luciano Boiteux, Milena Matto	Peo00751	Rio de Janeiro	Brazil	n/a
11.Luciano Boiteux, Milena Matto	Peo00752	Rio de Janeiro	Brazil	n/a
12.Tomasz Wawrzyczek	Peo00756	Rybnik	Poland	36-25383
13.Tomasz Wawrzyczek	Peo00757	Rybnik	Poland	36-25383
14.Tomasz Wawrzyczek	Peo00759	Rybnik	Poland	36-25383
15.Tomasz Wawrzyczek	Peo00761	Rybnik	Poland	36-25383
16.Gerda Hauge	Peo00762	W. Pymble	Australia	02-231-6500
17.Gerda Hauge	Peo00763	W. Pymble	Australia	02-231-6500
18.David Panjaputra, Lie Tjen Kian	Peo00764	Bandung	Indonesia	303286
19.Gustavo A. Ortiz Serrano	Peo00765	Santafe de Bogota	Colombia	57-1-2104243
20.Holger Moller	Peo00766	Usingen	Germany	06081-12483
21.Michael Sassani	Peo00767	Silver Spring	U.S.A.	301-585-7604
22.Alice Carey	Peo00768	Crawfordsville	U.S.A.	317-364-0296
23.Leandro Marcio G. Mansano	Peo00769	Sao Paulo	Brazil	299-5026
24.Emmanuel D'Esparbes	Peo00770	Saint Gilles	France	262-240710
25.Hans-Peter Kauth	Peo00771	Hamburg	Germany	040-850-86-35
26.Diane Riggs	Peo00772	Carmichael	U.S.A.	916-483-7815
27.Stanislawa Dorbrzeniecka	Peo00774	Szczecin	Poland	48-91-526-043
28.Stanislawa Dorbrzeniecka	Peo00775	Szczecin	Poland	48-91-526-043
29.Richard Clothier	Peo00777	Windlesham	United Arab Emirates	01276-476-423
30.Robert Hammond	Peo00778	Bogart	U.S.A.	706-613-6974

People, Plants and Animals

Page 85

Designer	File Name	City	Country	Telephone Number
1.Robert Hammond	Peo00779	Bogart	U.S.A.	706-613-6974
2.George Flores	Peo00781	Irvine	U.S.A.	714-768-3709
3.George Bure	Peo00782	Peoria	U.S.A.	602-566-8248
4.Emma Childs	Peo00784	Torpoint	United Kingdom	01752 823464
5.Chas Lindermyer	Peo00786	Fair Oaks	U.S.A.	916-863-2520
6.Elsa Cals Brugger	Peo01383	Rio de Janeiro	Brazil	5521-325-2888
7.Jos Luiz Silva Prada	Peo01384	Santafe de Bogota	Columbia	252 62 07
8.Ken Dove	Peo00795	Calgary	Canada	403-274-6296
9.Ricardo Ademar Sanchez	Peo00798	Sao Paulo	Brazil	826-3066
10.Francesco Verdu	Peo00799	Mutxamel	Spain	96-565-9917
11.Tibirica Altamiro Dias	Peo00802	Belo Horizonte	Brazil	031-443-5829
12.Anders Leergberg	Peo00805	Solroed Strand	Denmark	see PG Stage
13.Richard Aydlett	Peo00806	Earlysville	Australia	804-985-2212
14.Guenther Grauel	Peo00808	Gudensberg	Germany	05603-3683
15.Robert Mason	Peo00809	Scarborough	Canada	416-751-9048
16.Azar Azeem	Peo00811	Roy	U.S.A.	801-773-3151
17.Sensini Almerys	Peo00816	Cesena	Italy	0547-330493
18.Robert A. McCoy	Peo00819	Pontiac	U.S.A.	815-844-3808
19.Eric Gauthier	Peo00820	Gharlesbourg	Canada	418-626-1322
20.Simone Pampado	Peo00826	Frassinelle	Italy	39-425-933-117
21.Barto Farrar	Peo00827	Fort Worth	U.S.A.	817-834-1162
22.Barto Farrar	Peo00828	Fort Worth	U.S.A.	817-834-1162
23.Giacomo Pirro	Peo00829	Martinengo	Italy	363-988-830
24.Thomas Penn	Peo01385	Akron	U.S.A.	216-794-8515
25.Alexey Pavlov	Peo01386	Ulyanovsk	Russia	7-8422-322529
26.Subkhan Khamidi	Peo01387	Yogyakarta	Indonesia	0274-586297
27.Sharon Dana	Peo01302	Milwaukee	U.S.A.	503-654-6021
28.Dave Fiedler	Peo01396	Harrah	U.S.A.	405-454-3993
29.David Panjaputra	Peo01399	Bandung	Indonesia	022-303286
30.Andre Feyaerts	Peo01402	Mijas	Spain	34-08-45-38-68

Page 86

Designer	File Name	City	Country	Telephone Number
1.Giacomo Pirro	Peo00830	Martinengo	Italy	363-988-830
2.Alice Sutherland	Peo00835	Fremont	U.S.A.	510-657-8208
3.Nicki Salvin-Wight	Peo00836	Woodinville	U.S.A.	206-788-2415
4.Robert Olivares	Peo00839	Sun Valley	U.S.A.	818-768-1196
5.Erika Roller	Peo00844	Neulengbach	Austria	02772 546 07
6.Gunter Brecht	Peo00846	MeBkirk	Germany	07575-1499
7.Gerhard Haese	Peo00847	Bovenden	Germany	05593-1657
8.Silvio Bilang	Peo00848	Chur	Switzerland	081-241691
9.Wilfried Riske	Peo00852	Voerde	Germany	0281-43323
10.Stefan Lange	Peo00853	Oberdischingen	Germany	n/a
11.Annett Heinze	Peo00863	Lichte	Germany	036-701-60803
12.Helmut Niemann	Peo00865	Erfurt	Germany	0361-721-515
13.Helmut Niemann	Peo00866	Erfurt	Germany	0361-721-515
14.Friedrich Hatheyer	Peo00870	Braunau Am Inn	Austria	07722-65962
15.Gunther Kusch	Peo00873	Berlin	Germany	030-6927592
16.Rene Arlt	Peo00875	Berlin	Germany	030-721-3023
17.Christine Kersch	Peo00878	Bregenz	Austria	0043-5574-45009
18.Urs Bolliger	Peo00879	Zurich	Switzerland	01-462196
19.Thomas Wunderlich	Peo00880	Jena	Germany	03641-609-206
20.Mel & Paul Miller	Peo00883	Clinton	U.S.A.	301-856-8907
21.Steven Schilds	Peo00892	Burnaby	Canada	604-521-3070
22.David Bartholomew	Peo00893	Fishers	U.S.A.	317-849-1351
23.Jose Prada	Peo00894	Santafe de Bogota	Columbia	252 62 07
24.Carola Fromm	Peo00897	Berlin	Germany	030-144-592-53
25.Roger Bessette	Peo00898	St-Joseph du Lac	Canada	514-473-8119
26.Joyce Richardson	Peo00900	Arlington	U.S.A.	703-892-2661
27.Ilona Reiners	Peo00904	Bruhl	Germany	02232-22668
28.Ilona Reiners	Peo00906	Bruhl	Germany	02232-22668
29.Ilona Reiners	Peo00907	Bruhl	Germany	02232-22668
30.Ilona Reiners	Peo00909	Bruhl	Germany	02232-22668

Page 87

Designer	File Name	City	Country	Telephone Number
1.Vinay Ingle	Peo00913	Burlington	U.S.A.	617-229-2142
2.Ilona Reiners	Peo00916	Bruhl	Germany	02232-22668
3.Ansgar Schmitz-Veltin	Peo00919	Konstanz	Germany	07533-5934
4.Claudia Carius	Peo00921	Altena	Germany	02352-52821
5.Claudia Carius	Peo00922	Altena	Germany	02352-52821
6.Frank Deubert	Peo00923	Munich	Germany	n/a
7.Derek Donovan	Peo00925	Nacogdoches	U.S.A.	409-569-1671
8.Jason Coor	Peo00927	Lincoln	U.S.A.	402-477-9408
9.Ceri Lines	Peo00930	Hsinchu	Taiwan	886-35-239-210
10.Jorn Paessler	Peo00931	Erlangen	Germany	011-49-9131-602-987
11.Jorn Paessler	Peo00936	Erlangen	Germany	011-49-9131-602-987
12.Jorn Paessler	Peo00938	Erlangen	Germany	011-49-9131-602-987
13.Amanda Lincoln	Peo00940	Portland	U.S.A.	207-773-9553
14.Michael Schmidt	Peo00941	Fritzlar	Germany	05622-6417
15.Michael Schmidt	Peo00943	Fritzlar	Germany	05622-6417
16.Patrick Cain	Peo00944	Omaha	U.S.A.	402-455-9762
17.Manon La Badie	Peo00949	Montreal	Canada	514-982-2185
18.Paul Drabot	Peo00951	Bromley	United Kingdom	081 289 2911
19.Donna Fano	Peo00953	Belleville	Canada	613-966-2668
20.G. Philip Angel	Peo00957	Marietta	U.S.A.	404-565-6257
21.Michael Barnes	Peo00960	Canon City	U.S.A.	719-275-2102
22.Hal Pickavance	Peo00961	Duncan	Canada	604-748-7705
23.David Howells	Peo00963	Hampstead	U.S.A.	603-329-5213
24.Martin von Mendel	Peo00964	Schwabach	Germany	9122-14773
25.Robin Noel	Peo00973	Newark	U.S.A.	302-737-4591
26.Joseph Weibel	Peo00974	Soultz	France	89 74 18 79
27.John Drago	Peo00977	White Plains	U.S.A.	914-683-5537
28.Hans-Joachim Kardinal	Peo00979	Berlin	Germany	030-431-0306
29.David Troy	Peo00980	Birmingham	United Kingdom	021 705 9165
30.Darlene Emerick	Peo00981	Lakewood	U.S.A.	303-988-5705

LIST OF ENTRIES

People, Plants and Animals

Page 88

Designer	File Name	City	Country	Telephone Number
1. Simone Pampado	Peo00984	Frassinelle	Italy	39-425-933-117
2.	Peo00761			
3.Michele Hausman	Peo00987	Algonquin	U.S.A.	708-854-9060
4.Guy Brisebois	Peo00990	Chertsey	Canada	514-882-3786
5.Daniel Blatti	Peo00993	Zurich	Switzerland	141-1-3119371
6.Federico Maso	Peo00996	Quarto d'Altino	Italy	011-39-422-823087
7.Jovita Chow	Peo00997	Santa Monica	U.S.A.	310-458-9624
8.Peter Kwiatkowski	Peo00998	London	Canada	519-434-5785
9.Andrea Schmid	Peo01000	Winterthur	Switzerland	52-222-86 58
10.Caroline Dayton	Peo01021	Copperas Cove	U.S.A.	817-542-2028
11.Damiao Campos	Peo01027	Niteroi	Brazil	021-611 5896
12.Damiao Campos	Peo01028	Niteroi	Brazil	021-611 5896
13.Thomas Wunderlich	Peo01032	Jena	Germany	03641-609-206
14.Henk Wyniger	Peo01033	Marburg	Germany	06421-682019
15.Henk Wyniger	Peo01034	Marburg	Germany	06421-682019
16.Rupert Nothdurfter	Peo01037	Krimml	Austria	06564-327
17.David Panjaputra, Lie Tjen Kian	Peo01038	Bandung	Indonesia	303286
18.Sharon Bennett	Peo01039	Plymouth	United Arab Emirates	44-0-1752-66604
19.Jose Gonzalez	Peo01042	Hialeah	U.S.A.	305-558-2059
20.Joan L. Schwartz	Peo01046	Marina Del Rey	U.S.A.	310-306-2272
21.Mickaela S. Earle	Peo01047	Westminster	U.S.A.	303-457-0774
22.Urs Wegmann	Peo01048	Ukarumpa	Papua New Guinea	774497
23.UrsWegmann	Peo01049	Ukarumpa	Papua New Guinea	774497
24.Gary Crilley	Peo01059	Paraparaumv Beach	New Zealand	04-298-5279
25.Ming Yau Cheuk	Peo01061	New York	U.S.A.	212-227-818 1
26.Francisco Ponce Rodolfo	Peo01064	Haedo	Argentina	659-3646
27.Bob Ugiansky	Peo01065	Silver Spring	U.S.A.	301-588-9540
28.Milena Maia de Mattos	Peo01066	Rio de Janeiro	Brazil	512 3577
29.Marcus Abrahao	Peo01073	Rio de Janeiro	Brazil	55-21-2339814
30.Diane Riggs	Peo01081	Carmichael	U.S.A.	916-483-7815

Page 89

Designer	File Name	City	Country	Telephone Number
1.Diane Riggs	Peo01081	Carmichael	U.S.A.	916-483-7815
2.Hannes Stepper	Peo01083	Berg	Germany	09189-7381
3.Nico & Raphaela Hanke	Peo01084	Brunn/Geb.	Austria	0043/2236/34164
4.Volodymyr Kharchenko	Peo01086	Kiev	Ukraine	7-044-543-6335
5.Volodymyr Kharchenko	Peo01088	Kiev	Ukraine	7-044-543-6335
6.Rupert Nothdurfter	Peo01090	Krimml	Austria	06564-327
7.Nicki Salvin-Wight	Peo01092	Woodinville	U.S.A.	206-788-2415
8.B. Wieriks	Peo01093	Vlaardingen	Netherlands	010-435-0246
9.Norbert W. ChaussT	Peo01095	Sykesville	U.S.A.	410-549-1506
10.Monica Day	Peo01102	Oakville	Canada	905-827-6250
11.Elsa Cals Brugger	Peo01104	Rio de Janeiro	Brazil	5521-325-2888
12.Stanislawa Dobrzeniecka-Zylkowska	Peo01110	Szczecin	Poland	4891/526043
13.Stanislawa Dobrzeniecka-Zylkowska	Peo01112	Szczecin	Poland	4891/526043
14.Sharleen Sy	Peo01115	Toronto	Canada	416-755-5347
15.Michele Adamson	Peo01119	White Plains	U.S.A.	914-948-1629
16.Luz Earley	Peo01120	Irving	U.S.A.	214-438-3907
17.Ranaldo Ray	Peo01121	Cap-Rouge	Canada	418-651-2002
18.Ranaldo Ray	Peo01122	Cap-Rouge	Canada	418-651-2002
19.Anthony Rezendes	Peo01123	Austin	U.S.A.	512-469-7445
20.Lillian Peng	Peo01124	San Jose	U.S.A.	408-428-0228
21.Rosanna Stefanelli	Peo01128	Anzio	Italy	39-6-9865444
22.Elana Tontini	Peo01130	Anzio	Italy	39-6-9865444
23.Elana Tontini	Peo01131	Anzio	Italy	39-6-9865444
24.Dr. Hector Berumen Felix	Peo01133	Aguascalientes	Mexico	
25.Mary Hargis	Peo01135	Indianapolis	U.S.A.	317-484-8358
26.Roman Pietruszka	Peo01147	Kreuztal	Germany	+49 2732 27723
27.Darrell Gilmore	Peo01150	Parksville	Canada	
28.P. Parkinson	Peo01151	Chadderton	England	01616781314
29.Hans Christian Hildenbrand	Peo01153	Iserlohn	Germany	02371-12589
30.Guido Grassi	Peo01154	Genova	Italy	10-200716

Page 90

Designer	File Name	City	Country	Telephone Number
1.Mike Zdancewicz	Peo01158	Katy	U.S.A.	713-392-2331
2.Dan Daulby	Peo01160	Richmond	Canada	604 279-9536
3.Eric K. Wallis	Peo01162	Logan	U.S.A.	801-750-0327
4.Michael Degen	Peo01166	Heinsberg	Germany	49-2452-21110
5.David Huss	Peo01173	Austin	U.S.A.	512-835-0112
6.Larry Leszczewicz	Peo01175	Chicago	U.S.A.	312 890-1883
7.Kathleen Pratt	Peo01176	Fremont	U.S.A.	510 651-3585
8.Joseph Dreslinski	Peo01177	Smyrna	U.S.A.	404-431-4728
9.Michael Spollen	Peo01178	Horsham	United Kingdom	215-657-8600
10.Lie Tjeng Kian	Peo01180	Bandung	Indonesia	62-22-303-286
11.Jill Hotchkiss	Peo01185	Reva	U.S.A.	
12.Filho Salomao	Peo01191	Sao Paulo	Brazil	011-881-2448
13.Filho Salomao	Peo01192	Sao Paulo	Brazil	011-881-2448
14.Filho Salomao	Peo01193	Sao Paulo	Brazil	011-881-2448
15.Filho Salomao	Peo01194	Sao Paulo	Brazil	011-881-2448
16.Claude Grenier	Peo01196	Ste-Cecile de Whitton	Canada	819-583-3980
17.Filho Salomao	Peo01197	Sao Paulo	Brazil	011-881-2448
18.Filho Salomao	Peo01199	Sao Paulo	Brazil	011-881-2448
19.Filho Salomao	Peo01200	Sao Paulo	Brazil	011-881-2448
20.Filho Salomao	Peo01201	Sao Paulo	Brazil	011-881-2448
21.David Howse	Peo01203	St. John's	Canada	709 738-1053
22.Ashley Newell	Peo01204	St. John's	Canada	709 738-1053
23.Luiz Claudio Souza da Costa	Peo01205	Rio de Janeiro	Brazil	55-021-228-5669
24.Roman Alvarez Fidalgo	Peo01212	D. F.	Mexico	(5) 5-49-54-66
25.Roman Alvarez Fidalgo	Peo01213	D. F.	Mexico	(5) 5-49-54-66
26.Mauro/Laura Blasi/Cultrera	Peo01214	Rome	Italy	
27.Donald Warren	Peo01216	Jacksonville	U.S.A.	904-355-2745
28.Pawel Bodytk	Peo01221	Colleyville	U.S.A.	817 421-1150
29.Conrado Murguia	Peo01224	Cuernavaca	Mexico	73-13-82-52
30.John Maurer	Peo01229	Atlanta	U.S.A.	404-264-5392

People, Plants and Animals

Page 91

Designer	File Name	City	Country	Telephone Number
1.Barbara M. Lopez	Peo01231	TPA	U.S.A.	813-287-2740
2.Jose Edson da Costa	Peo01235	Fortaleza	Brazil	085-228-4241
3.Gregor Nussberger	Peo01239	Miami	U.S.A.	305 271-0075
4.Supharb Ratanalerthada	Peo01242	Bangkok	Thailand	066-2-377-6316
5.Katy Velazco-Lopez	Peo01244		U.S.A.	512-854-4733
6.Ojel E. Rodriguez Rivera	Peo01246	San Juan	Puerto Rico	809-792-1900
7.Nina J. Bramble	Peo01247	Tuncurry	Australia	065-545 549
8.Heidi Ronne	Peo01249	Trondheim	Norway	47-73 50 24 87
9.Mark Stanczyk	Peo01250	Glasgow	Scotland	041-649-9268
10.Dejan Nukic	Peo01251	Vienna	Austria	043-1-3320018
11.Thom Pettit	Peo01252	Lufkin	U.S.A.	409-634-8744
12.Randy Marks	Peo01254	Monterey	U.S.A.	408-372-0358
13.Petronio Cunha	Peo01257	Olinda	Brazil	081-429-0059
14.Petronio Cunha	Peo01259	Olinda	Brazil	081-429-0059
15.Teddi Deppner	Peo01275	Lincoln	U.S.A.	916-645-9092
16.Dany Babushkin	Peo01279	Sofia	Bulgaria	00359-2-598-384
17.Dany Babushkin	Peo01280	Sofia	Bulgaria	00359-2-598-384
18.Dany Babushkin	Peo01287	Sofia	Bulgaria	00359-2-598-384
19.Dany Babushkin	Peo01288	Sofia	Bulgaria	00359-2-598-384
20.Francesco Accardo	Peo01292	Lugano	Switzerland	0041-91-57-51-86
21.Alan Belcher	Peo01293	San Antonio	U.S.A.	210-492-6977
22.Carol/Chris Wright	Peo01300	Rosburg	U.S.A.	503-440-6814
23.Caroline Dayton	Peo01301	Copperas Cove	U.S.A.	817-542-2028
24.Lillian Peng	Peo01313	San Jose	U.S.A.	408-428-0228
25.Jan Myr Johnson	Peo01315	Portland	U.S.A.	503 283-4453
26.Marjo Degens	Peo01321	Heerlen	Netherlands	031 45 211990
27.Marjo Degens	Peo01322	Heerlen	Netherlands	031 45 211990
28.Rhonda S. Keene	Peo01323	Poughquag	U.S.A.	914-724-5156
29.Jean-Louis Mazzia	Peo01326	Bedarrides	France	90 33 04 61
30.Ryszard/Juliusz Bukanski/Piechocki	Peo01329	Gorzow WLKP	Poland	095-324-176

Page 92

Designer	File Name	City	Country	Telephone Number
1.Stefano Braam	Peo01330	Burgh-Haamstede	Netherlands	01115-3962
2.Michael Thomas	Peo01331	Oak Park	United States	708-386-2461
3.Adim Martin Ebube	Peo01332	Hyattsville	U.S.A.	301-699-8528
4.Diana Bloemendal	Peo01335	Kozenburg	Netherlands	01019-18877
5.Joe C. Werner	Peo01340	Pleasant Hill	U.S.A.	510-228-3522
6.GTrard Loncle	Peo01342	Mennecy	France	64 99 65 75
7.Rory Simpson	Peo01344	Oshawa	Canada	905-434-1335
8.Stanislawa Dobrzeniecka-Zylkowska	Peo01346	Szczecin	Poland	4891-526043
9.Stanislawa Dobrzeniecka-Zylkowska	Peo01348	Szczecin	Poland	4891-526043
10.Bardos Attila	Peo01349	Velpke	Germany	5364-4533
11.Bardos Attila	Peo01350	Velpke	Germany	5364-4533
12.Dalia Levin	Peo01353	Rehovot	Israel	972-8-466795
13.Dejan Nukic	Peo01354	Vienna	Austria	043-1-3320018
14.Willem Zwaard	Peo01405	Abcoude	The Netherlands	02946-3204
15.Dalia Levin	Peo01406	Rehovot	Israel	972-8-466795
16.Remi Forcier	Peo01409	Vancouver	Canada	604-685-7696
17.Lucie Prihodova	Peo01412	Zdar	Czech Republic	0042-616-27-939
18Jesse Mesa Toves	Peo01414	Agana	U.S.A.	671-637-1272
19.Finn Halskov	Peo01417	Tranbjerg J.	Denmark	89455513
20.Min Lee	Peo01422	Toronto	Canada	416-693-8783
21.Min Lee	Peo01423	Toronto	Canada	416-693-8783
22.Dagmar Freidrich	Peo01424	Munich	Germany	49 89-64 06 55
23.Terry Horton	Peo01425	Kansas City	U.S.A.	816-734-4808
24.Joan L. Schwartz	Peo01428	Marina Del Rey	U.S.A.	310-306-2272
25.Jolanta Romanowska	Peo01431	Warsaw	Poland	24-38-69
26.Himanshu Sud	Peo01432	New Delhi	India	91-11-6848715
27.Himanshu Sud	Peo01434	New Delhi	India	91-11-6848715
28.Daniel Wonham	Peo01436	Thunder Bay	Canada	807-344-5139
29.Gerry Wilson	Peo01404	Brooklyn	U.S.A.	718 836 9181

Page 93

Designer	File Name	City	Country	Telephone Number
1.Tanja Schellig	Peo01357	Berlin	Germany	030-2807163
2.Stanislawa Dobrzeniecka-Zylkowska	Peo01358	Szczecin	Poland	4891/526043
3.Victoria E.Riley	Peo01359	Cincinnati	U.S.A.	513-742-5691
4.Hans Pete r Kauth	Peo01360	Hamburg	Germany	040-850-86-35
5.Hans Peter Kauth	Peo01361	Hamburg	Germany	040-850-86-35
6.Sharleen Sy	Peo01362	Toronto	Canada	416-755-5347
7.Jerome C .Gunnell	Peo01363	New York	U.S.A.	718-876-1088
8.W. Wayne Frick	Peo01364	Staunton	U.S.A.	n/a
9.Matthijs Van Leeuwen	Peo01365	Enschede	Netherlands	31 53 760 969
10.HervT Lambinet	Peo01366	Paris	France	16 1 49 25 57 06
11.Steffen Brandt	Peo01369	Apolda	Germany	n/a
12.Robert Gagnon	Peo01370	Cobble Hill	Canada	604-743-4237
13.Terry Horton	Peo01372	Kansas City	U.S.A.	816-734-4808
14.Loretta Lombardy	Peo01373	St. Cloud	U.S.A.	407-892-3177
15.Luiz Eduardo de Oliveira	Peo01376	Rio de Janeiro	Brazil	21-294-8756
16.John Taylor	Peo01377	Essex	United Kingdom	0181-593-8837
17.Ojel E. Rodriguez Rivera	Peo01380	San Juan	Puerto Rico	809-792-1900
18.Virgilio Wallis Carvalho	Peo01381	Oeiras	Portugal	351-1-4570805
19.Siegfried Putz	Peo00519	Perlesreut	Germany	08555-691
20.Virgilio Wallis Carvalho	Peo01382	Oeiras	Portugal	351-1-4570805
21.Elsa Cals Brugger	Peo01383	Rio de Janeiro	Brazil	5521-325-2888
22.Francesco Vavassori	Peo00021	Bonate Sotto	Itlaia	035-99-3555
23.Dalia Levin	Peo01353	Rehovot	Israel	972-8-466795
24.Attila Bardos	Peo01350	Velpke	Germany	5364-4533
25.Stanislawa Dobrzeniecka-Zylkowska	Peo01110	Szczecin	Poland	4891-526043

Landscapes, Landmarks and Abstracts

Page 94

Designer	File Name	City	Country	Telephone Number
1.Mohr Gunther	Lan00007	Magdeburg	Germany	
2.Rodriguez Daniel	Lan00009	Buenos Aires	Argentina	361-4736
3.Mejia Ray	Lan00031	Indianapolis	U.S.A.	317-923-7808
4.Schisas Nick	Lan00037	Queensland	Australia	07-264-1025

Landscapes, Landmarks and Abstracts

Page 94

Designer	File Name	City	Country	Telephone Number
5.Hawk Chris	Lan00053	Boulder	U.S.A.	303-880-4295
6.Donato Richard	Lan00055	Chicago	U.S.A.	312-427-4520
7.Sito Beatrice	Lan00063	Washington	U.S.A.	202-473-1529
8.Glucz Michael	Lan00068	Victoria	Australia	59-750-339
9.Forcier Remi	Lan00073	Vancouver	Canada	604-685-7696
10.Seth Martin	Lan00094	Gifhorn	Germany	
11.Stevenson Crawford Russell	Lan00095	Tayside	United Kingdom	577-864-776
12.Lopatka Piotr	Lan00096	Ostrow Wielkopos	Poland	064-36-75-71
13.Frits W. Godin	Lan00086	Harbour City	U.S.A.	310-830-0175
14.Fassbinder Fritz	Lan00113	Ulm	Germany	49-731-385-904
15.Jones Bruce W.	Lan00116	Atlanta	U.S.A.	404-875-1517
16.McCormick Peter	Lan00117	Sun City West	U.S.A.	602-584-8403
17.Tomaselli Enrico	Lan00134	Rome	Italy	214-7909
18.Kardinal Hans-Joachim	Lan00136	Berlin	Germany	030-431-0306
19.McCoy Robert A.	Lan00167	Pontiac	U.S.A.	1-815-844-3808
20.Ushev Theodor	Lan00503	Sofia	Bulgaria	359-2-65-88-51
21.Baker Anne	Lan00505	Springfield	U.S.A.	217-787-1521
22.Le Tran Huan	Lan00509	Toronto	Canada	819-778-6750
23.Romanowska Jolanta	Lan00514	Warsaw	Poland	24-38-69
24.Kardinal Hans-Joachim	Lan00524	Berlin	Germany	030-431-0306
25.Kardinal Hans-Joachim	Lan00525	Berlin	Germany	030-431-0306
26.Cross James C.	Lan00527	Houston	U.S.A.	713-999-7076
27.Rommel Kenneth C.	Lan00537	Freeport	U.S.A.	516-546-3641
28.Godin Frits W.	Lan00543	Harbour City	U.S.A.	310-830-0175
29.Dobrzeniecka-Zylkowska Stanislawa	Lan00550	Szczecin	Poland	4891-526043
30.Dobrzeniecka-Zylkowska Stanislawa	Lan00551	Szczecin	Poland	4891-526043

Page 95

Designer	File Name	City	Country	Telephone Number
1.Rene Arlt	Lan00565	Berlin	IGermany	030-721-3023
2.Peter McCormick	Lan00577	Sun City West	U.S.A.	602-584-8403
3.Hans-Joachim Kardinal	Lan00586	Berlin	Germany	030-431-0306
4.Fabrice Geelen	Lan00652	Liege	Belgium	041-442-668
5.Jim Newman	Lan00667	Clearwater	U.S.A.	813-461-7962
6.Donna Wandel	Lan00689	Derby	U.S.A.	203-734-1369
7.Montserrat Noguera Muntadas	Lan00694	Barcelona	Spain	487-1280
8.Kevin Gilbertson	Lan00728	Shoreview	U.S.A.	612-484-7034
9.Bruce Kelton	Lan00744	Poulsbo	U.S.A.	360-779-3796
10Angela Schall	Lan00795	Fellbach	Germany	0711-589-124
11.Friedrich Ranz	Lan00805	Seibersdorf	Austria	43-2254-780-3854
12.Wil Dawson	Lan00820	Tulsa	U.S.A.	918-234-1362
13.Piotr Lopatka	Lan00840	Ostrow Wielkopolski	Poland	064-36-75-71
14.Hans Christian Hildenbrand	Lan00872	Iserlohn	Germany	02371-12589
15.Hal Pickavance	Lan00876	Duncan	Canada	604-748-7705
16.Cris Ticar	Lan00904	Mississauga	Canada	905-896-4664
17.Gunther Mohr	Lan00943	Magdeburg	Germany	
18.Theodor Ushev	Lan00944	Sofia	Bulgaria	359-2-65-88-51
19.Hans-Joachim Kardinal	Lan00950	Berlin	Germany	030-431-0306
20.Remi Forcier	Lan00968	Vancouver	Canada	604-685-7696
21.Jesse Mesa Toves	Lan01050	Agana	U.S.A.	671-637-1272
22.Alessandro Saccardo	Lan01053	Thiene	Italy	039-445-361939
23.Montserrat Noguera Muntadas	Lan01063	Barcelona	Spain	487-1280
24.David Huss	Lan01135	Austin	U.S.A.	512-835-0112
25.Robert A. McCoy	Lan01138	Pontiac	U.S.A.	1-815-844-3808
26.Eduardo Salgado Christensen	Lan01170	Montevideo	Uruguay	5982-796852
27.Bob Therrien	Lan01175	New Haven	U.S.A.	203-776-6279
28.Huan Le Tran	Lan01213	Aylmer	Canada	819-778-6750
29.Petronio Cunha	Lan01218	Olinda	Brazil	081-429-0059
30.Fred van Wijk	Lan01259	Zaltbommel	Netherlands	04180-14728

Page 96

Designer	File Name	City	Country	Telephone Number
1.Rod Macdonald	Lan01332	Vancouver	Canada	604-685-7696
2.Winfried Brandt	Lan01335	Southfield	U.S.A.	810-352-2345
3.Alice Mininch	Lan00014	Pleasant Hill	U.S.A.	510-228-3522
4.Alice Mininch	Lan00023	Rio de Janeiro	Brazil	21-294-8756
5.Alice Mininch	Lan00028	Hildesheim	Germany	05121-12821
6.Guilio Girolami	Lan01033	Singapore	Rep. of Singapore	65-344-1269
7.Scott J. Hamlin	Lan00039	Berlin	Germany	49-306-061766
8.David GagnT	Lan00064	Aarhus	Denmark	86 10 7370
9.Terry Horton	Lan00065	Pleasant Hill	U.S.A.	510-228-3522
10.Morton J. Litwack	Lan00066	Pleasant Hill	U.S.A.	510-228-3522
11.Himanshu Sud	Lan00077	Cesena	Italy	0547-330493
12.Himanshu Sud	Lan00079	London	Canada	519-471-3069
13.Himanshu Sud	Lan00080	London	Canada	519-471-3069
14.Raymond Brizzi	Lan00082	Berlin	Germany	030-9320277
15.David Thomas	Lan00088	Warsaw	Poland	24-38-69
16.Michael Ferguson	Lan00089	Bremgarten	Switzerland	57-37-76-26
17.Barry J. Gould	Lan00090	Bremgarten	Switzerland	57-37-76-26
18.Tamas Hajas	Lan00092	Schoonrewoerd	Holland	31-3454-2115
19.Marijke de Wendt	Lan00093	Gifhorn	Germany	
20.Reed/Linda Fisher/Calberg				
21.Maz Grimm	Lan00095	Kinross	Scotland	577-864-776
22.Francesc Pastor 1 Verdu	Lan00962	Chertsey	Canada	514-882-3786
23.Gustavo A. Ortiz Serrano	Lan00097	Buenos Aires	Argentina	541-923-7946
24.Donald Warren	Lan00100	Buenos Aires	Argentina	541-923-7946
25.Francesco Vavassori	Lan00101	Frankfort	U.S.A.	502-875-4460
26.Francesco Vavassori	Lan00103	Huntsville	U.S.A.	205-539-0186
27.Allan Weatherall	Lan00104	Brighton	U.S.A.	303-452-1039
28.Victoria E. Riley	Lan00105	Brighton	U.S.A.	303-452-1039
29.Michael Degen	Lan00106	Brighton	U.S.A.	303-452-1039
30.Christos Nussli	Lan00107	Harbour City	U.S.A.	310-830-0175

Page 97

Designer	File Name	City	Country	Telephone Number
1.Ruthie Nultemeier	Lan00611	Londonderry	U.S.A.	603-432-9899
2.Danny Chambers	Lan00612	Hackensack	U.S.A.	201-641-7150
3.Peter Schaefer	Lan00613	Dortmund	Germany	0231-469450

LIST OF ENTRIES

Landscapes, Landmarks, and Abstracts

Page 97

Designer	File Name	City	Country	Telephone Number
1.Ruthie Nultemeier	Lan00611	Londonderry	U.S.A.	603-432-9899
2.Danny Chambers	Lan00612	Hackensack	U.S.A.	201-641-7150
3.Peter Schaefer	Lan00613	Dortmund	Germany	0231-469450
4.Jose Luis P. Finneiredo	Lan00614	Rio de Janeiro	Brazil	n/a
5.Samer Al-Hunaty	Lan00615	Bad Friedrichshall	Germany	07136-22171
6.Samer Al-Hunaty	Lan00616	Bad Friedrichshall	Germany	07136-22171
7.Stephan Sprick	Lan00620	Dusseldorf	Germany	0211-253-633
8.Felix Kern	Lan00622	Eschborn	Germany	06196-42446
9.Bev Harcus	Lan00628	Langley	Canada	604-533-5854
10.Attila Bardos	Lan00629	Velpke	Germany	05364-4533
11.Roger Bessette	Lan00631	St-Joseph du Lac	Canada	514-473-8119
12.Frank Roth	Lan00646	Hunstetten 2	Germany	06126-8989
13.Marcelo Caula	Lan00651	Richmond	Canada	604-277-1874
14.Jonathon Watkins	Lan00656	Edinburgh	Scotland	031-449-6607
15.Richardo Cateriano Zapater	Lan00658	Lima	Peru	0051-14-222702
16.Aivars E. Perkons	Lan00659	Ottawa	Canada	613-737-7370
17.Daniel F Otth	Spe1026	Zurich	Switzerland	01-711-3170
18.Jurgen Schumacher	Lan00672	Berlin	Germany	030-9320277
19.Aguinaldo Pacheco	Lan00675	Vicosa	Brazil	55-31-891-3544
20.Michael Grenz	Lan00677	Schwindegg	Germany	08082-8116
21.Jolanta Romanowska	Lan00678	Warsaw	Poland	24-38-69
22.J.C. Boisvert	Lan00690	Nepean	Canada	613-823-1072
23.Montserrat Noguera Muntadas	Lan00694	Barcelona	Spain	487-1280
24.Marc C. Leydecker	Lan00696	Gloucester	U.S.A.	804-693-0189
25.Luiz Eduardo de Oliveira	Lan00698	Rio de Janeiro	Brazil	21-294-8756
26.Milton Padilla	Lan00699	Portland	U.S.A.	503-771-2690
27.Dwight S. Fisher	Lan00705	Raleigh	U.S.A.	919-878-4560
28.Fritz Fassbinder	Lan00706	Ulm	Germany	49-731-385-904
29.Richard Bruce Aydlett	Lan00707	Earlysville	Australia	804-985-2212
30.Zach Bakich	Lan00708	Toronto	Canada	416-533-7041

Page 98

Designer	File Name	City	Country	Telephone Number
1.Giacomo Pirro	Lan00709	Martinengo	Italy	363-988-830
2.Ray Trygstad	Lan00714	Naperville	U.S.A.	708-778-7443
3.Robert A. McCoy	Lan00715	Pontiac	U.S.A.	815-844-3808
4.Michael Hadac	Lan00718	Abbotsford	Canada	604-859-8168
5.Alice Mininch	Lan00719	Nepean	Canada	613-727-5696
6.Eric Moss	Lan00721	Harrogate	United Kingdom	423 525 807
7.Richard Donato	Lan00729	Chicago	U.S.A.	312-427-4520
8.Richard Donato	Lan00730	Chicago	U.S.A.	312-427-4520
9.Robert Hammond	Lan00734	Bogart	U.S.A.	706-613-6974
10.Jose Gonzalez	Lan00737	Hialeah	U.S.A.	305-558-2059
11.Phillippa Britton	Lan00740	Swansea	United Kingdom	01792 815591
12.David Lukin	Lan00745	Port Lincoln	Australia	86-824655
13.Pablo Javier Estevez	Lan00748	Resistencia	Argentina	54-722-22246
14.Adam Cole	Lan00749	Toronto	Canada	416-783-2233
15.Pascale Sasson	Lan00750	Montreal	Canada	514-485-7260
16.Michael J. Barnes	Lan00752	Canon City	U.S.A.	719-275-2102
17.Ray Williams	Lan00754	Longview	U.S.A.	360-577-4374
18.William Chin	Lan00757	Davao City	Philippines	221-6715
19.Carlo Doneda	Lan00758	Bergamo	Italy	035-31-33-33
20.Enrique Rosenthal	Lan00759	Montebello	U.S.A.	213-722-1311
21.Rob Bird	Lan00763	Kenilworth	United Kingdom	01926 58042
22.Xavier Bisbe	Lan00764	Torroella de Montgri	Spain	72-75-72-54
23.Richard Donato	Lan00766	Chicago	U.S.A.	312-427-4520
24.Ray Williams	Lan00767	Longview	U.S.A.	360-577-4374
25.Ivan Juric	Lan00770	Budapest	Hungary	361-1555-560
26.Ivan Juric	Lan00774	Budapest	Hungary	361-1555-560
27.Ivan Juric	Lan00777	Budapest	Hungary	361-1555-560
28.Pedro de Souza Silva	Lan00778	Rio de Janeiro	Brazil	55-21-252-8167
29.Pedro de Souza Silva	Lan00779	Rio de Janeiro	Brazil	55-21-252-8167
30.Linky De Bruyn	Lan00782	Waterkloof Park	South Africa	27-12-469-646

Page 99

Designer	File Name	City	Country	Telephone Number
1.Gerald Sittig	Lan00896	Furstenberg	Germany	05271-14995
2.Jurgen Plattmann	Lan00898	Dortmund	Germany	0231-174-002
3.Ulrich Bertelt, Nikola Bjelic	Lan00900	Bonn	Germany	0228-636-785
4.Paul D. Miller	Lan00902	Clinton	U.S.A.	301-856-8907
5.R.H., Schonfisch, Sr.	Lan00903	Redwood City	U.S.A.	415-365-5985
6.Ralf Wiencke	Lan00905	Dortmund	Germany	0231-721-2510
7.Harald W. Furche	Lan00906	Hamburg	Germany	040-636-3461
8.Karola Reimann	Lan00912	Bremen	Germany	0421-498-6186
9.Dagmar Friedrich	Lan00919	Munich	Germany	089-640-655
10.Heinz Nntzel	Lan00920	Bayreuth	Germany	0921-82727
11.Thomas Franzl	Lan00921	Karlstetten	Austria	n/a
12.H. Morgan Hicks	Lan00925	Seattle	U.S.A.	206-763-4427
13.	Lan01001			
14.David Howie	Lan00928	Toronto	Canada	416-751-2063
15.Karl-Heinz Eitner	Lan00929	Springe	Germany	05041-4147
16.Michael Schmidt	Lan00930	Fritzlar	Germany	05622-6417
17.Gary Barnett	Lan00931	Chatham	Canada	519-351-3181
18.Pirjo Kytola	Lan00933	Tampere	Finland	358-31-222 6711
19.Marijke de Wendt	Lan01390	Haarlem	Netherlands	023-313424
20.Marijke de Wendt	Lan01391	Haarlem	Netherlands	023-313424
21.Bev Harcus	Lan00937	Langley	Canada	604-533-5854
22.Miloslav Kalab	Lan00938	Ottawa	Canada	613-993-6002
23.Ron Kramer	Lan00940	Glassport	U.S.A.	412-678-7569
24.Carlos Henrique Lopez, Jr.	Lan00945	Sao Paulo	Brazil	055-011-667578
25.Loris Sinanian	Lan00948	Lawndale	U.S.A.	310-214-5495
26.Hans-Joachim Kardinal	Lan00949	Berlin	Germany	030-431-0306
27.Mark Phipps	Lan00955	Bridgeton	USA	314-298-3500
28.Ferry Kuntoaji	Lan00959	Semarang	Indonesia	024-472673
29.Guy Brisebois	Lan00961	Chertsey	Canada	514-882-3786
30.Guy Brisebois	Lan00962	Chertsey	Canada	514-882-3786

Landscapes, Landmarks, and Abstracts

Page 100

Designer	File Name	City	Country	Telephone Number
1.Pedro de Souza Silva	Lan00122	Rio de Janeiro	Brazil	55-21-252-8167
2.Lynn Harriet	Lan00123	Concord	U.S.A.	510-682-5334
3.Lynn Harriet	Lan00124	Concord	U.S.A.	510-682-5334
4.Francisco Baerga	Lan00129	Bronx	U.S.A.	718-597-4451
5.Francisco Baerga	Lan00131	Bronx	U.S.A.	718-597-4451
6.Francisco Baerga	Lan00132	Bronx	U.S.A.	718-597-4451
7.Francisco Baerga	Lan00133	Bronx	U.S.A.	718-597-4451
8.Hans-Joachim Kardinal	Lan00136	Berlin	Germany	030-431-0306
9.Roanne Baldwin	Lan00137	Arlington	U.S.A.	703-534-5150
10.Michael Degen	Lan00138	Heinsberg	Germany	49-2452-21110
11.Jay B. Keen	Lan00140	Poughquag	U.S.A.	914-724-5156
12.Ken Colwell	Lan00142	Dorchester	Canada	506-379-6779
13.B.J. Moore	Lan00143	Shelbyville	U.S.A.	615-684-7820
14.Ernst Steinheimer	Lan00144	Oestrich-Winkel	Germany	06723-2767
15.Ernst Steinheimer	Lan00145	Oestrich-Winkel	Germany	06723-2767
16.Jochen Baumm	Lan00146	Lehrte	Germany	05132-56157
17.Carsten Fritschi	Lan00152	Hilzingen	Germany	07731-69973
18.Jurgen Weinert	Lan00153	Halle	Germany	49 345 5220975
19.Brian Lukis	Lan00154	Prior Lake	U.S.A.	612-447-2730
20.Gerry Wilson	Lan00159	Brooklyn	U.S.A.	718 836 9181
21.Robert Rasmussen	Lan00160	Skanderborg	Denmark	86 510351
22.Peter Ashley	Lan00161	Portland	U.S.A.	207-780-0305
23.Robin Hebert	Lan00164	Redding	U.S.A.	916-244-5673
24.	Lan00177			
25.	Lan00178			
26.	Lan00181			
27.	Lan00182			
28.	Lan00184			
29.	Lan00185			
30.	Lan00186			

Page 101

Designer	File Name	City	Country	Telephone Number
1.Mary E. Somerville	Lan00519	Chicago	U.S.A.	n/a
2.Robert Kaplan	Lan00520	Atlanta	U.S.A.	404-938-5416
3.Don Stevenson	Lan00526	Beaconfield	Canada	514-695-4223
4.Michael J. Barnes	Lan00533	Canon City	U.S.A.	719-275-2102
5.Wanda McNeil	Lan00539	Balto	U.S.A.	410-327-1295
6.Palle Pedersen	Lan00540	Karslunde	Denmark	45-421-51619
7.Jean Maurice Dennery	Lan00544	Vanier	Canada	613-824-5272
8.Gerald L. Nutter	Lan00546	St. George	U.S.A.	913-494-2014
9.Stanislawa Zylkowska	Lan00549	Szczecin	Poland	4891/526043
10.Siegfried Putz	Lan00522	Perlesreut	Germany	08555-691
11.Wolfgang Mueller	Lan00555	Vienna	Austria	43-160-47-346
12.Wolfgang Mueller	Lan00557	Vienna	Austria	43-160-47-346
13.Carol Robeson	Lan00558	Woodburn	U.S.A.	503-981-4328
14.Frank C. Geisler	Lan00559	Hercules	U.S.A.	510-724-6059
15.Mauricio Orellana	Lan00561	Sun Valley	U.S.A.	818-982-0332
16.Heinrich Weilhard	Lan00563	Karlsruhe	Germany	n/a
17.Christa Reisinger	Lan00564	Himmelried	Switzerland	n/a
18.Juergen Andersen	Lan00567	Hamburg	Germany	040-654-6816
19.Peter Schaefer	Lan00568	Dortmund	Germany	0231-469450
20.Peter Schaefer	Lan00569	Dortmund	Germany	0231-469450
21.Ralf Nehrkorn	Lan00570	Kaltenkirchen	Germany	04191-60467
22.Michael Schmidt	Lan00573	Fritzlar	Germany	05622-6417
23.Dennis Schroder	Lan00576	Hamburg	Germany	040-550-7652
24.Robin West	Lan00578	Port Elizabeth	South Africa	041-511021
25.Andreas Rose	Lan00596	Bremervorde	Germany	04764-1022
26.Eric Gauthier	Lan00598	Gharlesbourg	Canada	418-626-1322
27.Gabriel Bergeron	Lan00599	Sherbrooke	Canada	819-569-5833
28.Rodolfo Francisco Ponce	Lan00600	Haedo	Argentina	659-3646
29.Rodolfo Francisco Ponce	Lan00604	Haedo	Argentina	659-3646
30.Marijke de Wendt			Netherlands	023-313424

Page 102

Designer	File Name	City	Country	Telephone Number
1.Guy Brisebois	Lan00963	Chertsey	Canada	514-882-3786
2.Marijke de Wendt	Lan01385	Haarlem	Netherlands	023-313424
3.Eduino J. Pereira	Lan00966	Wheaton	U.S.A.	301-649-4307
4.Eduino J. Pereira	Lan00967	Wheaton	U.S.A.	301-649-4307
5.Alessandra Miola	Lan00970	Quarto d'Altino	Italy	011-39-422-824713
6.	Lan00532			
7.Ralph C. Lucas	Lan00979	Huntington Beach	U.S.A.	n/a
8.Christos Nussli	Lan00980	Yverdon	Switzerland	41 24-221350
9.Sharlene Holliday	Lan00981	Princeton	U.S.A.	609-639-2472
10.Markus Koote	Lan00983	Oberhausen	Germany	0208-677993
11.Thomas Wunderlich	Lan00984	Jena	Germany	03641-609-206
12.Thomas Wunderlich	Lan00985	Jena	Germany	03641-609-206
13.Veronika Aretz	Lan00988	Herzogenrath	Germany	49-2407-1579
14.Mark Mikrut	Lan00990	Leesburg	U.S.A.	904-353-8066
15.Emanuele Aschiero	Lan00991	Caronno Pert.	Italy	02-965-0718
16.Albert Sy Santos	Lan00995	Makati	Philippines	632-833-7109
17.Thomas Penn	Lan00998	Akron	U.S.A.	216-794-8515
18.Johannes Grunbaver	Lan01000	Krummennaab	Germany	n/a
19.Ken Farrar	Lan01004	Kamloops	Canada	604-828-0440
20.Linky De Bruyn	Lan01007	Waterkloof Park	South Africa	27-12-469-646
21.Linky De Bruyn	Lan01008	Waterkloof Park	South Africa	27-12-469-646
22.Robert Hammond	Lan01010	Bogart	U.S.A.	706-613-6974
23.Marijke de Wendt	Lan01388	Haarlem	Netherlands	023-313424
24.Veijo Lahtinen	Lan01012	Tampere	Finland	358-31-222-0711
25.Thea Menagh	Lan01015	Toronto	Canada	416-488-3372
26.Bill Purdell	Lan01020	Honolulu	U.S.A.	808-833-8528
27.Bob Ugiansky	Lan01026	Silver Spring	U.S.A.	301-588-9540
28.Bob Ugiansky	Lan01028	Silver Spring	U.S.A.	301-588-9540
29.Guilio Girolami	Lan01030	Rome	Italy	39 6-810-5847
30.Lin Hsin Hsin	Lan01033	Singapore	Rep. of Singapore	65-344-1269

Landscapes, Landmarks, and Abstracts

Page 103

Designer	File Name	City	Country	Telephone Number
1.Lin Hsin Hsin	Lan01035	Singapore	Rep. of Singapore	65-344-1269
2.Lin Hsin Hsin	Lan01038	Singapore	Rep. of Singapore	65-344-1269
3.Marcus Abrahao	Lan01040	Rio de Janeiro	Brazil	55-21-2339814
4.Graham Peters	Lan01041	Charlotte	U.S.A.	704-344-1372
5.Graham Peters	Lan01042	Charlotte	U.S.A.	704-344-1372
6.Janice Bloyed	Lan01044	Fresno	U.S.A.	209-299-0051
7.Janice Bloyed	Lan01046	Fresno	U.S.A.	209-299-0051
8.Diane Riggs	Lan01048	Carmichael	U.S.A.	916-483-7815
9.Jesse Mesa Toves	Lan01050	Agana	U.S.A.	671-637-1272
10.Robin Hebert	Lan01052	Redding	U.S.A.	916-244-5673
11.Mike Mallorie	Lan01058	Sublimity	U.S.A.	503-769-2764
12.Montserrat Noguera Muntadas	Lan01062	Barcelona	Spain	487-1280
13.Ranaldo Ray	Lan01069	Cap-Rouge	Canada	418-651-2002
14.Shloime Henig	Lan01072	Brooklyn	U.S.A.	718-851-0162
15.Josef Prchal	Lan01074	Heideck	Germany	09177-9551
16.Josef Prchal	Lan01076	Heideck	Germany	09177-9551
17.Urvisha Mistry	Lan01084	Johannesburg	South Africa	011-403-4350
18.Gerd Wedemeier	Lan01096	Sittard	Netherlands	0031 46 585180
19.Roman Pietruszka	Lan01105	Kreuztal	Germany	49 2732 27723
20.Joette & Roanne Baldwin	Lan01111	Arlington	U.S.A.	703-534-5150
21.Monica Kiss	Lan01112	Kaindorf	Austria	0043-3452-85343
22.N. Qadir Khan	Lan01116	Toronto	Canada	416-364-9822
23.R.H. Schonfisch, Sr.	Lan01120	Redwood City	U.S.A.	415-365-5985
24.James-Michael Harlan	Lan01127	Southfield	U.S.A.	810-352-2345
25.Frits W. Godin	Lan01128	Harbor City	U.S.A.	310-830-0175
26.Brandon Warner	Lan01129	Sonoma	U.S.A.	707-939-9168
27.John Blatter	Lan01131	Surrey	Canada	604-585-6128
28.Joseph Dreslinski	Lan01141	Smyrna	U.S.A.	404-431-4728
29.Joseph Dreslinski	Lan01142	Smyrna	U.S.A.	404-431-4728
30.Lie Tjeng Kian	Lan01149	Bandung	Indonesia	62-22-303-286

Page 104

Designer	File Name	City	Country	Telephone Number
1.Carlos Antonio Cardoso Marra	Lan01151	Porto Alegre	Brazil	051-223-6462
2.Carlos Antonio Cardoso Marra	Lan01152	Porto Alegre	Brazil	051-223-6462
3.Regina M. Baranowski	Lan01153	Altamonte Springs	U.S.A.	407-767-8656
4.Mihajio Soc	Lan01158	Winnipeg	Canada	204-334-4162
5.Christine Eason	Lan01159	St. John's	Canada	709-738-1053
6.Luiz Claudio Souza da Costa	Lan01160	Rio de Janeiro	Brazil	55-021-228-5669
7.Luiz Claudio Souza da Costa	Lan01161	Rio de Janeiro	Brazil	55-021-228-5669
8.Raymond G. Cranford	Lan01162	St. John's	Canada	709-738-1053
9.Kathy Hudson	Lan01163	St. John's	Canada	709-738-1053
10.Conrado Murguia	Lan01167	Cuernavaca	Mexico	73-13-82-52
11.Edward Ott	Lan01168	Buffalo	U.S.A.	716-838-9062
12.Eduardo Salgado Christensen	Lan01169	Montevideo	Uruguay	5982 796852
13.David & Ursula Garcia	Lan01173	West Lafayette	U.S.A.	317-743-7571
14.Dave Wakelin	Lan01176	Turangi	New Zealand	00647-386-8491
15.Ruben Calimbas	Lan01178	Surrey	Canada	604-589-8221
16.Noemi Casset	Lan01181	Buenos Aires	Argentina	832-5709
17.Piotr Barszczowski	Lan01188	Tarnow	Poland	48-0-14-212-312
18.Piotr Barszczowski	Lan01189	Tarnow	Poland	48-0-14-212-312
19.Piotr Barszczowski	Lan01190	Tarnow	Poland	48-0-14-212-312
20.David Cadorette, Bill Stapledon	Lan01193	Nashua	U.S.A.	603-882-5037
21.Haris Sutanto	Lan01197	Jakarta	Indonesia	021 6592147
22.Joaquim Borges Martinez	Lan01200	Salvador	Brazil	055 071 233 9342
23.Ary Lati Franco	Lan01201	Mexico	Mexico	011-525-203-5436
24.Johanna Rakauski	Lan01204	Eau Claire	U.S.A.	616-944-1519
25.Phillip Klinefelter	Lan01205	Eden Prairie	U.S.A.	934-6773
26.Timothy G. Harrington	Lan01206	Olathe	U.S.A.	913-469-8700
27.Gary Tipton	Lan01207	Fairfield	U.S.A.	513-858-3342
28.Wayne F. Holly	Lan01209	St. John's	Canada	709-738-1053
29.Jose Simancas, Jose Bastidas	Lan01210	Barquismeto	Venezuela	58-51-511981
30.James L. Bendixen	Lan01211	Santa Maria	U.S.A.	805-922-3017

Page 105

Designer	File Name	City	Country	Telephone Number
1.Petronio Cunha	Lan01221	Olinda	Brazil	081-429-0059
2.J.C.H.M. (Hans) Heimeriks	Lan01225	Delfzyl	Netherlands	n/a
3.J.C.H.M. (Hans) Heimeriks	Lan01226	Delfzyl	Netherlands	n/a
4.Caco Rodriauez	Lan01227	Sao Paulo	Brazil	011-210-5882
5.Caco Rodriauez	Lan01228	Sao Paulo	Brazil	011-210-5882
6.Caco Rodriauez	Lan01229	Sao Paulo	Brazil	011-210-5882
7.Kevin Keck	Lan01230	Oakland	U.S.A.	510-763-2929
8.Charles LaFountain	Lan01231	Ft. Worth	U.S.A.	817-448-8080
9.Dany Babushkin	Lan01235	Sofia	Bulgaria	00359-2-598-384
10.Carlos Payno Sanchez	Lan01236	Mexico	Mexico	525-525 85 63
11.Hans-Joachim Kardinal	Lan01244	Berlin	Germany	030-431-0306
12.Carl Heath	Lan01246	Watauga	U.S.A.	817-281-5761
13.Mike Anderson	Lan01247	Aurora	U.S.A.	708-896-5451
14.H.B.J. Heusinkveld	Lan01248	Doetinchem	Netherlands	31-8340-25001
15.Brian L. Hollenbeck	Lan01249	Annandale	U.S.A.	908-638-6616
16.Albert Eger	Lan01250	Weiden	Germany	0961-22880
17.George Nagy	Lan01253	Budapest	Hungary	361-322-44-03
18.Wiko Haripahargio	Lan01256	Jakarta Timur	Indonesia	0251-240030
19.Jay Thornton	Lan01258	Godfrey	Canada	613-374-3431
20.Joao Francisco de Oliveira Dias	Lan01262	Rio de Janeiro	Brazil	247-35-30
21.Shawn Knapp	Lan01266	Bay City	United Kingdom	517 686 4770
22.Ryszard Bukanski	Lan01267	Gorzow WLKP	Poland	095-324-176
23.Jouni Ahava	Lan01273	Espoo	Finland	358-0-5093-272
24.Enrique R. Cerda	Lan01280	Montebello	U.S.A.	213-722-1311
25.Richard Venus	Lan01282	Glenelg North	Australia	618-294-3548
26.R.H. Schonfisch, Sr.	Lan01283	Redwood City	United States	415-365-5985
27.Tamas Hajas	Lan01376	Szeged	Hungary	36 62-434-519
28.Ojel E. Rodriguez Rivera	Lan01288	San Juan	Puerto Rico	809-792-1900
29.Juergen Andersen	Lan01289	Hamburg	Germany	040-654-6816
30.Kees de Winter	Lan01290	Heenvleit	Netherlands	011-31-1887-3208

LIST OF ENTRIES

LIST OF ENTRIES

LIST OF ENTRIES

LIST OF ENTRIES

LIST OF ENTRIES

Corporate Identification

LIST OF ENTRIES

LIST OF ENTRIES

Specialty and Leisure

Page 162

Designer	File Name	City	Country	Telephone Number
26.Lydia Greenfield	Spe00629	Devonport	Australia	04-231-363
27.Helmut Kempfer	Spe00631	Vienna	Austria	0222-604-4334
28.Karlheinz Glockner	Spe00633	Wiesbaden	Germany	n/a
29.Thomas Moller	Spe00640	Schleswig	Germany	04621-360393
30.Thomas Moller	Spe00641	Schleswig	Germany	04621-360393

Page 163

Designer	File Name	City	Country	Telephone Number
1.Scott Wizell	Spe00644	Las Vegas	U.S.A.	702-222-1896
2.Philip G. Angel	Spe00660	Marietta	U.S.A.	404-565-6257
3.Virginia L. Curtis	Spe00664	Fredericksburg	U.S.A.	703-373-5901
4.Shane Hunt	Spe00672	San Dimas	U.S.A.	909-592-8533
5.Canale Giuseppe	Spe00684	Alba	Italy	0173-363844
6.Kitisak Ratanalerthada	Spe00690	Bangkok	Thailand	066-2-377-6316
7.Harald Mittmann	Spe00707	Witzenhausen	Germany	05542-4932
8.Rene Ebert	Spe00722	Kamenz	Germany	03578-5821
9.Carolynn Cobb	Spe00724	Dallas	U.S.A.	214-296-4808
10.Carolynn Cobb	Spe00725	Dallas	U.S.A.	214-296-4808
11.Carolynn Cobb	Spe00726	Dallas	U.S.A.	214-296-4808
12.Natalie Chusainow	Spe00732	Berlin	Germany	n/a
13.Natalie Chusainow	Spe00734	Berlin	Germany	n/a
14.Ralf Kothe	Spe00736	Bremen	Germany	0421-833-526
15.Uwe Lange	Spe00738	Mulheim/Ruhr	Germany	0208-592-475
16.Michael Sweig	Spe00739	North Bay	Canada	705-472-9913
17.Dalibor Feuereisl	Spe00747	Praha 10	Czech Republic	n/a
18.Dalibor Feuereisl	Spe00749	Praha 10	Czech Republic	n/a
19.James-Michael Gregory Harlan	Spe00750	Southfield	U.S.A.	810-352-2345
20.Alexander Klinko	Spe00763	Bratislava	Slovakia	07 / 781 383
21.Alexander Klinko	Spe00765	Bratislava	Slovakia	07 / 781 383
22.Alexander Klinko	Spe00766	Bratislava	Slovakia	07 / 781 383
23.Bruce W. Funderburk	Spe00773	Charlotte	U.S.A.	704-333-9011
24.Tryfon Manolis	Spe00776	Thessaloniki	Greece	003031/316815
25.Stephen C. Pearson	Spe00778	Hereford	England	01432-268-280
26.Virgil Milan	Spe00790	Memphis	U.S.A.	901-332-3311
27.Chuck Jonkey	Spe00791	Glendale	U.S.A.	818-247-6219
28.Kyle Doll	Spe00794	Altoona	U.S.A.	715-836-6850
29.Daryl Xavier-Wellard	Spe00803	Kanata	Canada	613-599-1454
30.William Lutkus	Spe00805	Watertown	U.S.A.	203-274-4828

Page 164

Designer	File Name	City	Country	Telephone Number
1.Pedro van Can,Fionna Bottema	Spe00807	Meerssen	Netherlands	31-43-644432
2.Salah Benferroudj	Spe00808	Montreuil	France	68-55-62-92
3.Salah Benferroudj	Spe00812	Montreuil	France	68-55-62-92
4.M.A. Humphreys	Spe00817	Exeter	United Kingdom	0392-468-484
5.Jose Simancas	Spe00818	Barquisimeto	Venezuela	58-51-511-981
6.Marcel Cadotte	Spe00819	Montreal	Canada	514-277-9947
7.Oliveri Enrico	Spe00822	Campoligure	Italy	010/921245
8.Jacopo Pirro	Spe00825	Martinengo	Italy	0363/9888 30
9.John Blatter	Spe00826	Surrey	Canada	604-585-6128
10.Janet Lee	Spe00829	Vancouver	Canada	604-222-8372
11.Fritz Fassbinder	Spe00830	Ulm	Germany	49-731-385-904
12.Alex Hoy	Spe00835	Solbjerg	Denmark	45-86-92-8366
13.Alex Hoy	Spe00836	Solbjerg	Denmark	45-86-92-8366
14.Ray Trygstad	Spe00840	Naperville	U.S.A.	708-778-7443
15.Bill Mogensen	Spe00843	Sunland	U.S.A.	818-352-4102
16.Dick Lim Yew Ling	Spe00854	n/a	Singapore	754-5577
17.Alice Mininch	Spe00855	Nepean	Canada	613-727-5696
18.Henry Farrar	Spe00859	Reading	United Kingdom	44-734-345211
19.David Gagn T.	Spe00863	London	Canada	519-663-9115
20.Isabel Gagn T.	Spe00864	London	Canada	519-663-9115
21.Joe A. Westrum	Spe00865	Florence	U.S.A.	803-663-1490
22.Marylou Baffoni	Spe00866	Fullerton	U.S.A.	714-870-4356
23.Enrique Rosenthal	Spe00869	Montebello	U.S.A.	213-722-1311
24.Marin Darmonkow, Neil Ellis	Spe00870	St. John's	Canada	709-747-0140
25.Marin Darmonkow, Neil Ellis	Spe00874	St. John's	Canada	709-747-0140
26.Janusz Wojciechowski	Spe00876	Kew Gardens	U.S.A.	718-441-1286
27.Tom Orr	Spe01745	Tarpon Springs	U.S.A.	813-942-9608
28.Lois G. Sullivan	Spe00878	Hinsdale	U.S.A.	603-256-6736
29.Lee Musick	Spe00879	Indianapolis	U.S.A.	317-290-0500
30.Lee Musick	Spe00880	Indianapolis	U.S.A.	317-290-0500

Page 165

Designer	File Name	City	Country	Telephone Number
1.Oliveri Enrico	Spe00822	Campoligure	Italy	010-921245
2.Jerome Sanderson	Spe00883	Indianapolis	U.S.A.	317-924-2990
3.Michael Schuster	Spe00884	Leingarten	Germany	n/a
4.Tom G. Lunzer	Spe00890	Vernon Hills	U.S.A.	708-634-6700
5.Diana Lien	Spe00892	Calgary	Canada	403-238-2740
6.Jennifer Schutts-Stone	Spe00903	Tampa	U.S.A.	813-622-8727
7.Victoria R. Kobayashi	Spe00906	Anaheim	U.S.A.	714-527-0529
8.Victoria R. Kobayashi	Spe00907	Anaheim	U.S.A.	714-527-0529
9.Paul Bean	Spe00911	Waterloo	Canada	519-746-2918
10.David Lukin	Spe00914	Port Lincoln	Australia	86 824655
11.Ray Williams	Spe00915	Longview	U.S.A.	360-577-4374
12.Theodore Artz	Spe00917	Philadelphia	U.S.A.	215-427-1954
13.Paul Norman	Spe00920	Norwich	United Kingdom	0603 872611
14.Herbert A. Lyon	Spe00921	Tampa	U.S.A.	813-839-3898
15.John Sparks	Spe00922	Louisville	U.S.A.	502-636-2790
16.Jonathon Epstein	Spe00926	Kent	U.S.A.	216-678-3534
17.Shawn Barone	Spe00936	Pgh	U.S.A.	412-327-8671
18.Andre Casualt	Spe00937	Orleans	Canada	613-830-3703
19.David Panjaputra,Lie Tjen Kian	Spe00940	Bandung	Indonesia	303286
20.Thomas Ossendorf	Spe00944	Bindlach	Germany	09208-57886
21.Joachim Flügel	Spe00945	Alling	Germany	08141-72695
22.Beverly Esch	Spe00946	Ravenna	U.S.A.	216-325-1040
23.Beverly Esch	Spe00948	Ravenna	U.S.A.	216-325-1040
24.Keith J. Howes	Spe00951	Limassol	Cyprus	0357-5-324-334
25.Keith J. Howes	Spe00953	Limassol	Cyprus	0357-5-324-334
26.Nada Mancevic	Spe00957	Ljubljana	Slovenia	386-61-556-260
27.Simon Koyounian	Spe00958	London	Canada	519-434-5785
28.Tryfon Manolis	Spe00962	Thessaloniki	Greece	003031/316815
29.Ron Jordan	Spe00963	El Cajon	U.S.A.	619-654-8240
30.Franz Meindl	Spe00967	Munich	Germany	49-89-837-977

Specialty and Leisure

Page 166

Designer	File Name	City	Country	Telephone Number
1.Georgann Gelsi-Piccirillo	Spe00964	Oakland	U.S.A.	201-476-3604
2.Janet Kirschen	Spe00979	Larkspur	U.S.A.	415-924-6975
3.Mark Ensinger	Spe00981	Novi	U.S.A.	810-348-8191
4.Rose Stefani-Guenther	Spe00983	E. Moline	U.S.A.	309-755-2300
5.Heinz Jung	Spe00985	Mehlingen	Germany	06303-1625
6.Matthias Gleirscher	Spe00987	Neustift	Austria	05226-2600
7.Joe C. Werner	Spe00988	Pleasant Hill	U.S.A.	510-228-3522
8.Andre Feyaerts	Spe00992	Mijas	Spain	34-08-45-38-68
9.Joseph Ackerman	Spe00999	Fresh Meadows	U.S.A.	212-283-5758
10.Rene Riedlinger	Spe01000	Houston	U.S.A.	713-690-8333
11.Terry Horton	Spe01001	Kansas City	U.S.A.	816-734-4808
12.Mariana Slemenson	Spe01002	Buenos Aires	Argentina	00541-785-6296
13.Sandra Lather-Benson	Spe01008	Oakland	U.S.A.	510-428-1305
14.William Figie	Spe01015	Cocoa	U.S.A.	407-632-7162
15.Martin Siegel	Spe01016	Akron	U.S.A.	216-972-7389
16.Ernest W. Richardson	Spe01018	Warner	Canada	403-642-2028
17.Piotr Lopatka	Spe01020	Ostrow Wielkopolski	Poland	064-36-75-71
18.Piotr Lopatka	Spe01021	Ostrow Wielkopolski	Poland	064-36-75-71
19.Giacomo Pirro	Spe01022	Martinengo	Italy	363-988-830
20.Giacomo Pirro	Spe01023	Martinengo	Italy	363-988-830
21.Daniel F. Otth	Spe01026	Zurich	Switzerland	01-711-3170
22.Guilio Girolami	Spe01029	Roma	Italy	39 6-810-5847
23.Randy Compas	Spe01030	Etobicoke	Canada	416-620-9315
24.Randy Compas	Spe01032	Etobicoke	Canada	416-620-9315
25.Nicki Salvin-Wight	Spe01034	Woodinville	U.S.A.	206-788-2415
26.Uwe Cochanski	Spe01035	Berlin	Germany	030-512-4039
27.Tobias Graning	Spe01036	Dieburg	Germany	06071/25889
28.Tobias Graning	Spe01038	Dieburg	Germany	06071/25889
29.Kristine Pachler	Spe01044	Bregenz	Austria	
30.Jasmin Hamacher	Spe01049	Kornwestheim	Germany	07154-180734

Page 167

Designer	File Name	City	Country	Telephone Number
1.Richard Donato	Spe01067	Chicago	U.S.A.	312-427-4520
2.William M. Colony	Spe01071	West Glacier	U.S.A.	406-387-5842
3.P. Basnett	Spe01072	Birkenhead	United Kingdom	44 151 608 1980
4.Michael Charness	Spe01074	Hunstville	U.S.A.	205-880-2277
5.Christine Kersch	Spe01081	Bregenz	Europe	0043-5574-45009
6.Thomas Wunderlich	Spe01088	Jena	Germany	03641-609-206
7.Kuno Gross	Spe01092	Koblenz	Germany	n/a
8.Nicole Ledoux	Spe01094	Yorktown Heights	U.S.A.	914-245-6938
9.Lothar Blenk	Spe01097	Bischofsmais	Germany	09920-570
10.Ronald Golemba	Spe01100	Toronto	Canada	416-699-6162
11.Fancesco Visona	Spe01104	Pisa	Italy	0039-050-560766
12.Marco Antonio Moncada	Spe01815	Mexico City	Mexico	603 05 15
13.Buz Mormann	Spe01814	N. Billerica	U.S.A.	508-670-5555
14.Sandra Puschmann	Spe01110	Lippstadt	Germany	02941-720258
15.Sandra Puschmann	Spe01111	Lippstadt	Germany	02941-720258
16.Sandra Puschmann	Spe01112	Lippstadt	Germany	02941-720258
17.Sandra Puschmann	Spe01113	Lippstadt	Germany	02941-720258
18.Jeff Stabinsky	Spe01114	Norwalk	U.S.A.	203-866-1002
19.Jenny Powlen	Spe01115	Indianapolis	U.S.A.	313-770-4259
19.Jenny Powlen	Spe01116	Indianapolis	U.S.A.	313-770-4259
20.Leonard W. Lopez	Spe01123	Apple Valley	U.S.A.	619-242-3341
22.Pierre Tremblay	Spe01124	St-Emile	Canada	418-842-5633
23.Petr Somel	Spe01125	St-Emile	Canada	418-842-5633
24.Jock Grant	Spe01128	Marianske Lazne	Czech Republic	42 165 4235
25.Michael Jablonski	Spe01132	Helensburgh	Scotland	01436 672450
26.Montserrat Noguera Muntadas	Spe01135	Chula Vista	U.S.A.	619-426-6928
27.Cesar E. Uson	Spe01137	Barcelona	Spain	487-1280
28.Irene McMillan	Spe01140	Edmonton	Canada	403-461-6945
29.Chris Purcell	Spe01145	San Diego	U.S.A.	619-259-0691
30.Terry Horton	Spe01051	Houston	U.S.A.	713-374-4679

Page 168

Designer	File Name	City	Country	Telephone Number
1.Roanne Baldwin	Spe01149	Arlington	U.S.A.	703-534-5150
2.Sensini Almerys	Spe01152	Cesena	Italy	0547-330493
3.Larry Green	Spe01154	Grayslake	U.S.A.	708-223-2426
4.Blanka Proksova,Zdenek Proks	Spe01166	Praha 5	Czech Republic	0042-2-558643
5.Daniel Blatti	Spe01167	Zurich	Switzerland	141-1-3119371
6.Galen Bolin	Spe01181	Charlotte	U.S.A.	704-376-6423
7.Ed Contalves	Spe01185	West Lorne	Canada	519-768-1414
8.Doug Thornton	Spe01189	Camarillo	U.S.A.	805-482-9885
9.Rick Gillan	Spe01194	Westminster	U.S.A.	n/a
10.Markus Koote	Spe01196	Oberhausen	Germany	0208-677993
11.Jari - Pekka Makinen	Spe01197	Turku	Finland	1358-21-2327742
12.Gary P. Ellis	Spe01201	Hesperia	U.S.A.	707-425-4862
13.Veronika Aretz	Spe01203	Herzogenrath	Germany	49-2407-1579
14.Rainer Mullner	Spe01208	Berghulen 2	Germany	07344-8444
15.David Panjaputra	Spe01211	Bandung	Indonesia	022-303286
16.Emanuele Aschiero	Spe01212	Caronno Pert.	Italy	02-965-0718
17.Michael Richard	Spe01214	Ventura	U.S.A.	805-643-4257
18.Benno Kiehl	Spe01216	Lohr	Germany	09352-5957
19.Bill Sharkey	Spe01217	Richmond Hill	Canada	416-480-4961
20.Judy Unger	Spe01220	Placentia	U.S.A.	714-993-1770
21.Terry Horton	Spe01221	Kansas City	U.S.A.	816-734-4808
22.Erwin Zettlmeier	Spe01224	Hengersberg	Germany	09901-6572
23.Erwin Zettlmeier	Spe01225	Hengersberg	Germany	09901-6572
24.Carol E. Farmer	Spe01228	Sterling	U.S.A.	703-481-2984
25.Peter Kwiatkowski	Spe01233	London	Canada	519-434-5785
26.Susan Rodgers	Spe01235	Pittsburgh	U.S.A.	412-922-4225
27.Peter van Heulen	Spe01245	Westkapelle	Netherlands	31-1187-2267
28.Peter van Heulen	Spe01246	Westkapelle	Netherlands	31-1187-2267
29.Linda/Thom Hildbold	Spe01255	Royal Oak	U.S.A.	810-280-1545
30.Zoran Damceski	Spe01260	Prilep	Macedonia	389 98 25 532

Page 169

Designer	File Name	City	Country	Telephone Number
1.Diego Sala	Spe01261	Agrate	Italy	39-039-6899791
2.Thea Menagh	Spe01269	Toronto	Canada	416-488-3372
3.Thea Menagh	Spe01272	Toronto	Canada	416-488-3372
4.	Spe01278			
5.Bob Ugiansky	Spe01289	Silver Spring	U.S.A.	n/a
6.Nazan Kucukcezzar	Spe01290	Silver Spring	U.S.A.	301-588-9540

Specialty and Leisure

Page 169

Designer	File Name	City	Country	Telephone Number
7.Peter Verdonck	Spe01292	Brabant	Belgium	32-2-377-58-27
8.Francis Rubin (Pflucker)	Spe01293	Lima	Peru	5114-447-4326
9.Francis Rubin (Pflucker)	Spe01295	Lima	Peru	5114-447-4326
10.Eric W. Harris	Spe01297	Santa Rosa	U.S.A.	707-542-2225
11.Colin Harrison	Spe01299	Melksham	United Kingdom	01225-707659
12.Colin Harrison	Spe01300	Melksham	United Kingdom	01225-707659
13.Corby W. Gorman	Spe01301	East Peoria	U.S.A.	309-699-2454
14.Alexander Klinko	Spe01302	Bratislava	Slovakia	07 / 781 383
15.Alexander Klinko	Spe01303	Bratislava	Slovakia	07 / 781 383
16.Chris Purcell	Spe01304	Houston	U.S.A.	713-374-4679
17.G. Boronat	Spe01307	Sale	United Kingdom	0161-905-2475
18.Manon La Badie	Spe01817	Montreal	Canada	514-982-2185
19.Choon Ean Goh	Spe01831	Austin	U.S.A.	512-444-2359
20.Winfried Brandt	Spe01836	Trier	Germany	0651-754-25
21.William R. Steele	Spe01318	Nashua	U.S.A.	603-888-5791
22.Tony & Anna Pace	Spe01319	Victoria	Canada	604-383-9353
23.Christoph Kellerman,Frank Hornig	Spe01321	Lunen	Germany	02036-73563
24.Wolfgang Schulz	Spe01322	Herrenberg	Germany	49-7032-34588
25.J.G. Hinojosa	Spe01323	Corpus Christi	U.S.A.	512-854-4733
26.Wendy Palmer	Spe01324	London	Canada	519-453-0585
27.David Mendes	Spe01326	Ariyo	Brazil	466-1868
28.Giacomo Pirro	Spe01333	Martinengo	Italy	363-988-830
29.Michael Oke	Spe01334	London	Canada	519-681-8620
30.Winfried Brandt	Spe01837	Trier	Germany	0651-754-25

Page 170

Designer	File Name	City	Country	Telephone Number
1.Paula K. Singer	Spe01336	Passaic	U.S.A.	201-472-0619
2.Ralf & Heike Taubert	Spe01340	Hann Munden	Germany	055411-12368
3.Ross Bartlett	Spe01344	Aylmer	Canada	819-684-4477
4.Ross Bartlett	Spe01349	Aylmer	Canada	819-684-4477
5.Luis E. Burgueno	Spe01354	Trelew	Argentina	0965-22108
6.Dominic Hilton	Spe01356	Johannesburg	South Africa	011-403-4350
7.Rory Mark	Spe01357	Johannesburg	South Africa	011-403-4350
8.Rory Mark	Spe01358	Johannesburg	South Africa	011-403-4350
9.Rory Mark	Spe01360	Johannesburg	South Africa	011-403-4350
10.Harshila Mistry	Spe01361	Johannesburg	South Africa	011-403-4350
11.Harshila Mistry	Spe01362	Johannesburg	South Africa	011-403-4350
12.Harshila Mistry	Spe01363	Johannesburg	South Africa	011-403-4350
13.Alain Eagles	Spe01367	Johannesburg	South Africa	011-403-4350
14.Alain Eagles	Spe01368	Johannesburg	South Africa	011-403-4350
15.Alain Eagles	Spe01369	Johannesburg	South Africa	011-403-4350
16.Natasha Matthews	Spe01370	Johannesburg	South Africa	011-403-4350
17.Natasha Matthews	Spe01371	Johannesburg	South Africa	011-403-4350
18.Marija Jerkovic	Spe01372	Johannesburg	South Africa	011-403-4350
19.Marija Jerkovic	Spe01373	Johannesburg	South Africa	011-403-4350
20.Mandy Palmer	Spe01374	Johannesburg	South Africa	011-403-4350
21.Michael Lloyd	Spe01376	Johannesburg	South Africa	011-403-4350
22.Michael Lloyd	Spe01377	Johannesburg	South Africa	011-403-4350
23.Jason Purshouse	Spe01378	Johannesburg	South Africa	011-403-4350
24.Jason Purshouse	Spe01379	Johannesburg	South Africa	011-403-4350
25.Anita Bhikha	Spe01380	Johannesburg	South Africa	011-403-4350
26.Anita Bhikha	Spe01381	Johannesburg	South Africa	011-403-4350
27.Michael Gene Adkins	Spe01382	Westville	U.S.A.	918-723-3190
28.Gail S. Bronstein	Spe01387	Gardnerville	U.S.A.	702-265-2748
29.William MacDonald	Spe01389	Phoenix	U.S.A.	602-438-0616
30.Russell Dove	Spe01395	Tucson	U.S.A.	520-888-9345

Page 171

Designer	File Name	City	Country	Telephone Number
1.Bobby Levow	Spe01396	New York	U.S.A.	212-473-7974
2.Shawn Schmidlen	Spe01397	Burnham	U.S.A.	717-242-4393
3.Luciano Boiteux,Gustavo Ventureni	Spe01398	Rio de Janeiro	Brazil	n/a
4.Hans Wang	Spe01402	Cambridge	U.S.A.	617-661-8514
5.Mary E. York	Spe01405	Ausgusta	U.S.A.	706-667-9344
6.Mary E. York	Spe01407	Ausgusta	U.S.A.	706-667-9344
7.Michael Degen	Spe01417	Heinsberg	Germany	49-2452-21110
8.Robert Buckner	Spe01420	Cottage Grove	U.S.A.	612 4589722
9.Scott P. Sullivan	Spe01421	Madison	U.S.A.	608-256-7225
10.Kathleen Pratt	Spe01424	Fremont	U.S.A.	510 651-3585
11.Antonin Malec	Spe01431	Ceske Budejovice	Czech Republic	42-38-38763
12.Manon-Lacramioara Toroc	Spe01435	Cluj-Napoca	Romania	40-641-85887
13.Llyn Strelau	Spe01436	Calgary	Canada	403-228-0644
14.Llyn Strelau	Spe01437	Calgary	Canada	403-228-0644
15.Manon-Lacramioara Toroc	Spe01438	Cluj-Napoca	Romania	40-641-85887
16.Manon-Lacramioara Toroc	Spe01440	Cluj-Napoca	Romania	40-641-85887
17.Virginia L. Curtis	Spe01445	Fredericksburg	U.S.A.	703-373-5901
18.Franco Chimienti	Spe01447	Caracas	Venezuela	02-7517268-712298
19.Franco Chimienti	Spe01448	Caracas	Venezuela	02-7517268-712298
20.Cordell Dietz	Spe01450	Boise	U.S.A.	208-345-2982
21.Cynthia Skorlinski	Spe01460	Charlotte	U.S.A.	704-525-6618
22.Mario Dacosta	Spe01461	Windsor	Canada	519-945-6588
23.Luis Pedro C. Ferreira	Spe01465	Porto Alegre	Brazil	55-51-233-4288
24.Luis Pedro C. Ferreira	Spe01467	Porto Alegre	Brazil	55-51-233-4288
25.Lilli Mathiesen	Spe01476	Berkhamsted	United Kingdom	01422- 877-650
26.Luis Eduardo Leon	Spe01481	Bogota	Colombia	2154-672
27.David Barker	Spe01482	North Canton	U.S.A.	216-490-4779
28.Piotr Barszczowski	Spe01486	Tarnow	Poland	48-0-14-212-312
29.Piotr Barszczowski	Spe01487	Tarnow	Poland	48-0-14-212-312

Page 172

Designer	File Name	City	Country	Telephone Number
1.Piotr Barszczowski	Spe01488	Tarnow	Poland	48-0-14-212-312
2.Donna Gattone	Spe01494	St. Augustine	U.S.A.	904-797-2600
3.Charlie Behre	Spe01495	Ft. Lauderdale	U.S.A.	305-328-1357
4.Joerg T. Fiederer	Spe01500	Panorama City	U.S.A.	818-893-4346
5.Fajar Hariyanto	Spe01538	Surbaya	Indonesia	6231 716202
6.Barbara Durham	Spe01544	Cleveland	U.S.A.	216-459-1690
7.Dant Musarra	Spe01545	Laguna Niguel	U.S.A.	1-800-289-7478
8.Cathy A. Reece	Spe01549	Memphis	U.S.A.	901-371-9182
9.Cathy A. Reece	Spe01550	Memphis	U.S.A.	901-371-9182
10.Cathy A. Reece	Spe01551	Memphis	U.S.A.	901-371-9182
11.Cathy A. Reece	Spe01552	Memphis	U.S.A.	901-371-9182
12.Cathy A. Reece	Spe01553	Memphis	U.S.A.	901-371-9182

LIST OF ENTRIES

Specialty and Leisure

Designer	File Name	City	Country	Telephone Number
Page 172				
1.Barbara Durham	Spe01555	Cleveland	U.S.A.	216-459-1690
2.Barbara Durham	Spe01556	Cleveland	U.S.A.	216-459-1690
3.Heidi Ronne	Spe01557	Trondheim	Norway	47-73 50 24 87
4.Werner Kramer	Spe01569	Schriesheim	Germany	0 6203-68559
5.Edward C. Hoar	Spe01578	Delaware	U.S.A.	614-369-1789
6.Lydia M. Cabico	Spe01579	Downey	U.S.A.	310-940-8211
7.John A. Crawford	Spe01582	Harpers Ferry	U.S.A.	304-725-5532
8.Petronio Cunha	Spe01585	Olinda	Brazil	081-429-0059
9.Wim Hein	Spe01593	Enschede	Netherlands	053-31 88 98
10.Angelo Manoel da Silva	Spe01602	Altinho	Brazil	081-722-4588
11.Dany Babushkin	Spe01604	Sofia	Bulgaria	00359-2-598-384
12.Roger Casselman	Spe01607	Ottawa	Canada	613-954-8847
13.Marcel Pierron	Spe01622	Sorgues	France	90 83 01 05
14.Monica Fortman, Edwina Arnold	Spe01624	Emmitsburg	U.S.A.	301-447-1138
15.Josef Prchal	Spe01635	Heideck	Germany	09177-9551
16.Josef Prchal	Spe01636	Heideck	Germany	09177-9551
17.Josef Prchal	Spe01637	Heideck	Germany	09177-9551
18.Marielle Liege	Spe01638	Voisins le BTX	France	1-3096-0236
Page 173				
1.Frederic Mommeja	Spe01640	La Barden	France	905-537-06
2.Petronio Cunha	Spe01643	Olinda	Brazil	081-429-0059
3.Joe Thomson	Spe01646	Las Vegas	U.S.A.	702-656-8738
4.Noor Khan	Spe01649	San Francisco	U.S.A.	415 292-5673
5.Giacomo Pirro	Spe01652	Martinengo	Italy	363-988-830
6.Elsa Cals Brugger	Spe01657	Rio de Janeiro	Brazil	5521-325-2888
7.Alun Rogers	Spe01660	Cardiff	United Kingdom	044 1222 874
8.Don Henrich	Spe01663	Waterloo	Canada	519-746-5595
9.Don Henrich	Spe01664	Waterloo	Canada	519-746-5595
10.Irv Boichuk	Spe01667	Gabriola	Canada	604-247-9887
11.Mel Mohan	Spe01670	Belleville	Canada	613-967-2823
12.Robert Hammond	Spe01671	Bogart	U.S.A.	706-613-6974
13.Josef Valek, Milan Matous	Spe01673	Valasske Mezirici 3	Czech Republic	42-651-21716
14.Josef Valek, Milan Matous	Spe01675	Valasske Mezirici 3	Czech Republic	42-651-21716
15.Josef Valek, Milan Matous	Spe01676	Valasske Mezirici 3	Czech Republic	42-651-21716
16.Laszlo Csizmadia	Spe01681	Pecsvarad	Hungary	36-72-465 757
17.William Lutkus	Spe01682	Watertown	U.S.A.	203-274-4828
18.William R. Clegg	Spe01688	Cayey	Puerto Rico	809-738-2751
19.Dejan Nukic	Spe01718	Vienna	Austria	043-1-3320018
20.Cristiano Albrecht	Spe01690	Porto Alegre	Brazil	051-330-1758
21.Cristiano Albrecht	Spe01692	Porto Alegre	Brazil	051-330-1758
22.Gerald L. Nutter	Spe01697	St. George	U.S.A.	913-494-2014
23.Sally Ainsworth	Spe01699	Cardiff	United Kingdom	01222 874271
24.Christos Nussli	Spe01703	Yverdon	Switzerland	41-24-221350
25.Michel Dupuis	Spe01706	St-Basile	Canada	514-653-6691
26.Michel Dupuis	Spe01707	St-Basile	Canada	514-653-6691
27.Tadeusz Szechowski	Spe01716	Nowa Sol	Poland	0-688-75438
28.Dalia Levin	Spe01717	Rehovot	Israel	972-8-466795
29.Paul Wicksteed	Spe01721	Nelson	New Zealand	03 5468561

Charity

Designer	File Name	City	Country	Telephone Number
Page 174				
1.Piotr Lopatka	Cha00018	Ostrow Wielkopolski	Poland	064-36-75-71
2.William R. Clegg	Cha00506	Cayey	Puerto Rico	809-738-2751
3.Luciano Boiteux	Cha00559	Rio de Janeiro	Brazil	n/a
4.W. Bruce Funderburk	Cha00567	Charlotte	U.S.A.	704-333-9011
5.Tomasz Wawrzyczek	Cha00576	Rybnik	Poland	36-25383
6.William R. Clegg	Cha00577	Cayey	Puerto Rico	809-738-2751
7.David Panjaputra	Cha00639	Bandung	Indonesia	022-303286
8.Stephen Arscott	Cha00642	Mississauga	Canada	905-896-4664
9.Linky De Bruyn	Cha00645	Waterkloof Park	South Africa	27-12-469-646
10.Mari T. E. Climent	Cha00650	Mutxamel	Spain	34-6-5659917
11.Alexander Klinko	Cha00652	Bratislava	Slovakia	07 781 383
12.Norbert W. Chausse	Cha00654	Sykesville	U.S.A.	410-549-1506
13.Bodo R. Lebbing	Cha00680	Borken	Germany	49-2861-64371
14.Georgina Curry, Gerry Moss	Cha00725	Scottsdale	U.S.A.	602-443-8786
15.Theodor Ushev	Cha00754	Sofia	Bulgaria	359-2-65-88-51
16.Fajar Hariyanto	Cha00763	Surbaya	Indonesia	6231 716202
17.	Cha00638			
18.Martin Grec	Cha00728	Humenne	Slovakia	42-933-5450

Corel Professional Photos

Designer	File Name	City	Country	Telephone Number
Page 175				
1.Tim Gorski	Pho00004	Fort Lauderdale	U.S.A.	305-463-7618
2.Theodor Ushev	Pho00504	Sofia	Bulgaria	359-2-65-88-51
3.Joshua R. Cline	Pho00508	Lake Milton	U.S.A.	216-654-5659
4.Ian Mountain	Pho00558	Romford	United Kingdom	850 138 926
5.Terry Sunday	Pho00612	EL Paso	U.S.A.	915-584-9301
6.Michael Koester	Pho00615	Goeppingen	Germany	49-7-161-42847
7.Michael John Hill	Pho00616	Umina	Australia	43-434-721
8.Ian Mountain	Pho00565	Romford	United Kingdom	850-138-926
9.Radim Mojzis	Pho00593	Vsetin	Czech Republic	42657-61 1336
10.Wojciech Pawelko	Pho00595	Lindenhurst	U.S.A.	516-254-6760
11.Franz Kanters	Pho00596	Boerdonk	Czech Republic	04929-62329
12.Jim Morriss	Pho00602	Rt 4 Roanoke	U.S.A.	817-491-4201
13.Jim Morriss	Pho00603	Rt 4 Roanoke	U.S.A.	817-491-4201
14.Kuapil Ales	Pho00605	C. Budejovice	Czech Republic	n/a
15.Kuapil Ales	Pho00606	C. Budejovice	Czech Republic	n/a
16.John & Peter Reddy	Pho00608	Dublin	Ireland	496-2000
17.Ralf Koehler	Pho00610	64293 Daritstadt	Germany	049-6151-294209
18.Terry Sunday	Pho00613	EL Paso	U.S.A.	915-584-9301
19.Jim Deitrich	Pho00617	French Camp	U.S.A.	209-983-1463
20.Adrian Brookes	Pho00001	Ottawa	Canada	613-596-4942
21.David Walsh	Pho00005	Brisbane	Australia	07-353-1529
22.Peter van Heulen	Pho00009	Westkapelle	Netherlands	31-1187-2267
23.Johan Widegren	Pho00507	Vasteras	Sweden	46-21-189-374
24.James Graham Edwards	Pho00510	Eumemmerring	Australia	03-794-9013
25.Thomas Quinn	Pho00536	Owners Grove	U.S.A.	708-832-0209
26.Paul M. Brooks	Pho00548	Folsom	U.S.A.	916-983-1050